# HOME RUNS
## — AND —
# STRIKEOUTS
## in a Social Enterprise

### A Leadership Memoir

## JAMES M. McCLELLAND

# DEDICATION

*To Jane, Scott, Diane, Claire, and Rachel*

# CONTENTS

# INTRODUCTION

Toward the end of my 41 years as CEO of what had become a large, diversified not-for-profit organization, I identified 104 significant initiatives we had taken during my career. Some were new ventures or services, some were significant variations on or extensions of something we were already doing, others were major process changes, and I classified them in baseball terms. There were ten home runs – eight with bases loaded, 18 strikeouts, a lot of singles, and a few doubles. But the impact of the eight home runs with bases loaded – those grand slam home runs - far exceeded the net cumulative impact of all the other initiatives.

There were two keys to this approach. One was having a board of directors that not only allowed us to exercise our entrepreneurial inclinations, but also allowed us to fail at some of what we tried and learn and grow from the experiences. The other key was ensuring that the risks we took were prudent and that we didn't bet too much on any one initiative. It also helped greatly that we had a lot of continuity in key positions at the board and upper management levels. That gave us a strong institutional memory, which helped keep us from repeating our mistakes. Of course, because we were entrepreneurial, we would make new ones. But that was OK as long as the risks were prudent.

The Indianapolis-based organization I led, Goodwill Industries of Central Indiana (now, because of a merger after I retired, Goodwill of Central and Southern Indiana) grew tremendously during those years, from less than $3 million to more than $130 million in annual revenue. The vast majority of that revenue was earned by selling products or providing services on contract or for a fee, and most of that was in a competitive marketplace. With 3,300 employees, we had become the 4th largest of 164 community based Goodwills in the U.S., while operating in the 33rd largest market. Moreover, all of that growth had been organic and within 29 central Indiana counties; no mergers or acquisitions had been involved.

The substantial growth, though, was not nearly as significant as how the organization had evolved to increase its long-term impact in the lives of people and the communities where we operated. The scope of services was much broader and offered opportunities to people with a wide variety of disabilities, low education levels, and/or involvement with the criminal justice system. In addition to 59 retail stores, we operated 12 public charter high schools with total enrollment of over 3,500 students, e-commerce and recycling operations, ten commercial services sites, and a nurse home visitation program for 600 first-time moms in low-income households. Two-thirds of our employees had limited options because of a disability, felony conviction within the previous ten years, and/or lack of a high school diploma. Half of those were the primary source of income in their households.

While we were viewed as a very successful organization, it certainly was not all smooth sailing. In this book I'll describe not only what worked, including some of the home runs, and some of what didn't work – the strikeouts. I'll also describe how we adapted over the years as the world around us changed in remarkable ways. And I'll describe some of the lessons I learned in a leadership role that was a nearly constant learning and growing experience for four decades.

In the title of this book, I refer to the organization I led as a social enterprise. Goodwill was one of the early social enterprises, as from its inception it has used a commercial means (the sale of used goods in a competitive marketplace) to accomplish a social mission. Throughout its history, Goodwill has earned the vast majority of its revenue from the sale of products and services.

In the early days, the mission was to provide work - opportunities for unemployed people to earn money so they could buy the basic necessities of life. That is still one of Goodwill's most important historic roles, as the organization provides jobs for many thousands of people whose options are limited by disability, low education levels, criminal histories, or other significant barriers. Goodwill also helps many individuals prepare for and find jobs with other employers. Early Goodwill slogans such as "Not alms, but opportunity," "Not charity, but a chance," and "A hand up, not a hand-out" are as applicable today as they were a century ago.

Today, most of the jobs Goodwill provides still revolve around the collection and sale of used merchandise. In the organization I led, 2,200 of our 3,300 employees were part of our retail division. In addition, though, Goodwills now collectively also employ thousands more in other mission-related, mostly self-sustaining operations.

I view the way and the extent to which Goodwill blends business with mission as one of the organization's most unique characteristics, and I frequently described our overall objective in general terms as "maximizing mission-related impact while maintaining a financial position that's good for the organization's long-term viability." Of course, that required us to define "impact" as well as possible. That was always a work-in-progress, with improvements in definition and performance over time.

Today there is a lot of debate over the primary purpose of a corporation. While the dominant theory over the past 50 years has defined that purpose as maximizing shareholder value, there has been growing support for recognizing the corporation as having a responsibility to also consider other stakeholders, including customers, employees, suppliers, and communities more than might have often been the case in the past.

It strikes me that some of the approaches we used in the organization I led for four decades are just as applicable in for-profit public benefit corporations as they are in not-for-profit organizations. Some of those approaches might also be useful in a sub-set of other for-profit companies that choose to increase their consideration of stakeholders other than shareholders. While no single approach works for all, some of the lessons from our experiences at Goodwill might be useful to many.

When I stepped down as CEO in 2015, I attributed the success of our organization to five key factors:

- Our people – a lot of smart, talented people who brought to their work not just their knowledge and skills, but also a strong commitment to the mission. In other words, they brought their heads and their hearts. And that is an unbeatable combination in an organization such as Goodwill.

- Our Board of Directors – a superb, highly engaged, but not micromanaging board that permitted experimentation and allowed for some of those experiments to fail. A related key factor was a consistently professional and productive relationship between the board and the CEO.

- The culture – characterized in part by a constant desire to find ways to further improve and increase long term impact in the lives of people and the communities where Goodwill operated. It was also a culture in which respect for others was paramount and people generally worked well together across departmental and divisional lines.

- Relationships – with a lot of people in a lot of other organizations across the for-profit, not-for-profit, and public sectors.

- A strong financial position – largely a result of a very successful donated goods/retail operation. An endowment that had grown to $30+ million by the time I retired had also been enormously helpful – especially as a source of seed money to help launch new mission-enhancing ventures and services.

The first three elements in that list were interrelated. I could not have led the organization the way I did without the kind of board we had and the relationship I had with the board over a long period of time. I go into this in some detail in Chapter 10. Of course, our people and the culture were closely interrelated. The culture helped attract a lot of our most talented and committed staff, and they in turn helped reinforce the culture.

To a significant degree, the relationships with people in other organizations and the strong financial position resulted from the other factors in that short list.

Throughout the book, I'll elaborate on each of these elements as I tell the story of how we grew and evolved. Interspersed among the chapters, I've also included several pieces I describe as *Food for Thought*. First, though, in Chapter 1 I will provide some additional background on Goodwill Industries and convey a bit more about my path into the organization.

# PART I

*Beginnings*

# OPENING THOUGHTS

## *The Magnificence of the Ordinary*

*While solutions to major social problems must be macro in scale, in the final analysis we must see results in the lives of individual people. As Peter Drucker reminded us, the ultimate purpose of a not-for-profit organization is to change lives.*

*As we offer opportunities to help others improve their lives, the changes can often be in ways that on the surface might seem unremarkable. As we look deeper, though, we discover that often they are really much more. Here are some brief sketches of a few people I've been fortunate to know.*

*Cheryl dropped out of high school. She came to Goodwill in the early 1970s, learned keyboard skills, got a GED, a driver's license, and a job. A few years later she got married, then had a son. The last time I saw her, she had been married for over 30 years, and their son had graduated from college. Cheryl worked nearly all her adult life until her husband retired.*

*Sounds pretty ordinary until you learn that Cheryl was born with no arms. When you know this, you begin to realize that there is nothing ordinary about Cheryl's life and that, in fact, what she has done with her life is truly magnificent.*

*Bobby had few opportunities – educational or otherwise - when he was growing up. After he began working at Goodwill, one of our staff helped him learn how to write his name and tell time. He was then 36 years old. For weeks after that, every time he would see me he would ask me if I knew what time it was. Then he would tell me. For most people, learning how to write your name and tell time are pretty ordinary accomplishments. For Bobby, though, they were magnificent achievements.*

*Steve was severely limited by cerebral palsy. He used a motorized wheelchair and communicated using a keyboard with a voice synthesizer. He worked for several years on a contract Goodwill had to do janitorial work in a large federal building in Indianapolis. With a broom attached to his wheelchair, Steve swept 1-1/2 miles of corridors every day. He absolutely loved his job and his co-workers, and they loved him.*

*One day, Steve was in his motorized wheelchair crossing a street. While he was in a marked crosswalk, a car hit him, killing him instantly.*

*Many people would not have considered a person doing such an ordinary – and to some, a menial – task to be a success. But Steve exceeded everyone's expectations – except possibly his own - and worked at a level many would never have thought possible. And he was happy doing it. For Steve, what to most people might have seemed so ordinary was truly magnificent.*

*When I started working for Goodwill, a member of our board of directors told me he thought Goodwill was amazing. The way he saw it, we took goods people no longer wanted and people no one else wanted to hire and combined them to create self-sustaining employment for a lot of people who otherwise would have been sitting at home surviving on public assistance. To him, ordinary household goods and ordinary people combined to produce something extraordinary and magnificent.*

*It's easy to get caught up in the busyness of day-to-day work and life and, in my case, take for granted a lot of what many of our people did so well day in and day out. Fortunately, though, when I saw examples such as those I've mentioned and many others, I was reminded that much of what we tend to think of as pretty ordinary is much more than that. In fact, much of it is truly magnificent.*

# CHAPTER 1
## Background

Well over 100 years ago, at the beginning of the 20th Century, Edgar Helms, a Methodist minister, saw a human need and developed a not-for-profit commercial means to fill that need and accomplish a societal "good." Seeking a practical way to help the thousands of unemployed immigrants in the south end slums of Boston in those days, Helms collected clothing, furniture, and household items people no longer wanted, put unemployed people to work repairing the goods, and sold them to the public. Money from the sales was used to pay wages to the workers. The organization he created, Goodwill Industries, is now composed of over 150 locally governed and managed community based not-for-profit organizations that collectively constitute one of the largest networks of charitable organizations in the world.

Each local Goodwill is a member of Goodwill Industries International, Inc. (GII) and operates within a GII-assigned geographic territory. While GII has certain requirements of all Goodwills, including how the name and marks may be used, the locals have almost complete freedom in how they operate, what services to provide, their policies and procedures, etc. The degree of autonomy each Goodwill has results in enormous variability from one Goodwill to another. They most definitely are not all alike.

This structure has advantages and disadvantages. Among the disadvantages are inconsistency in the scope of services offered and wide variation in performance from one locale to another. It is also enormously difficult to generate economies of scale that might be possible with a different structure.

On the other hand, independent community based Goodwills do have the ability to customize their services and approaches to best suit their community. They also have opportunities to learn a lot from the different approaches and experiences of other Goodwills. Importantly from my perspective, that freedom at the local level is what enabled the Indianapolis-based organization to evolve differently from any other Goodwill during the early years of the 21st Century.

The geographic limitations that are placed on each local Goodwill can also result in a tendency to over-diversify as a means of generating growth. Not all Goodwills do that, but as will become obvious later in this book, we did have that tendency – especially in the 1980s and into the 1990s. We didn't know what we couldn't do, and we tried many ways to grow our businesses. Through trial and error, though, we eventually arrived at what I viewed as an optimal, sustainable level of diversification that led to something approaching optimal impact.

I was CEO of that central Indiana Goodwill organization for more than four decades. However, if, when I graduated from Georgia Tech, anyone had told me I would spend 45 of the next 50 years working as an executive for Goodwill Industries, I would have considered them delusional. And if they had told me that this fifth-generation Floridian would spend nearly all those years living and working in Indianapolis, that would have removed all doubt. Yet, I cannot imagine a career that would have been a better fit with my value system and whatever abilities I might have. Neither can I imagine a city that would have been more supportive of what we were trying to do than was Indianapolis.

I have had a number of friends around the country who also found a great career fit with Goodwill. We have differed in backgrounds, temperaments, and leadership styles, and different paths led us to Goodwill. Yet, despite the differences, for those of us who served multiple decades as Goodwill CEOs, there was something unique about the fit. Part of it, I believe, is that most of us had some entrepreneurial instincts, and we loved having the opportunity to run businesses that had a strong mission component.

Peter Drucker wrote that most successful careers are not planned, and mine certainly wasn't. Drucker believed that most successful careers are generally a result of understanding what your values are, what you do well, what you don't do well, the kinds of situations you work best in, and the kinds of situations you don't work well in. Then you try to find a fit with all of that.

My path is a good example of what Drucker described, and I was extraordinarily fortunate to find at a relatively early age (26) what for me was a nearly ideal fit. I had the same position for the last 41 years of my career, but the job itself changed phenomenally. I believe organizations and their key people need to grow at about the same rate. If one gets too far ahead of the other, there will be problems. The organization I was privileged to lead and I personally generally kept pace with each other's growth – not always exactly in sync, but usually with positive results.

But while we grew a lot, we also evolved into something far better than I had even imagined. The resulting impact of the work we were doing was particularly significant during the fifteen years before I retired and made the last part of my career by far the most rewarding. I loved what our organization had become.

I've been in a lot of leadership positions in my life. In addition to being CEO of a large, diversified not-for-profit organization, I've served on the boards of a lot of other not-for-profit organizations at local, national, and international levels and chaired several of them. Included among those was a joint venture between a U.S.-based organization and a U.K.-based charity.

One of the ironies in my life, though, is that I never sought any of the paid or unpaid leadership positions I've had as an adult. The only leadership positions I ever really sought were in high school. Even when I first contacted Goodwill back in 1970, I was looking for a place where I could use my industrial engineering skills in a way that might give me the kind of personal satisfaction I had enjoyed doing some volunteer tutoring in the basement of a church in downtown Washington D.C. while I was completing my military service.

One reason Goodwill interested me was its emphasis on providing jobs for people who, because of their disabilities, had fewer options than most. That interest had been stimulated by an experience I had while living in Washington D.C. in the late 1960s – a time of much social ferment in the U.S. While there, I got to know people from all parts of the country – people who had different backgrounds, perspectives, and world views than I had grown up with. They read different books from those I typically read, and they caused me to ask questions about issues I had never really thought about. But the answers I got to some of those questions – sometimes from unexpected places – at times had a profound and lasting impact on me.

For example, my parents were living in the Orlando area, where my dad was an officer in a company that sold and serviced road building and construction equipment. One evening when I was home visiting my parents I somewhat naively asked my dad, "Tell me, what does your company do for society?" He calmly replied, "Well, for starters, we provide a livelihood for 125 people and their families." I felt about one foot tall and wondered how I could have been so dumb as not to see that. Subsequently, through what turned out to be a very long career with Goodwill, hardly a week went by that I didn't think about that incident, as the organization I led employed a lot of people who not only had limited options, but over half of them were the primary source of income in their households. That placed an enormous responsibility on those of us in leadership positions to run the organization as well as possible so we could continue providing a livelihood for all those people who were counting on us. And we did not take that responsibility lightly.

In 1970, though, that was still to come as I considered my employment options. Finally, after six months of recruitment by what was then Goodwill Industries of America and procrastinating by me, I agreed to enter Goodwill's then-two-year-long executive training program under the mentorship of Bill Lufburrow, CEO of the Houston Goodwill. That decision involved taking a 25% pay cut and turning down two other job offers, each of which would have paid me 40% more than Goodwill. I also made a four-year commitment to work for Goodwill.

That is probably not what most people would have done. But remember, I'm the fifth-generation Floridian who has subsequently made Indianapolis home for nearly five decades. I've frequently not gone the more conventional route, and I've never regretted that. It's probably not surprising that I don't recall getting any career advice when I was a kid. But I was so independent-minded I probably wouldn't have paid much attention to it anyway.

The driving force behind my decision to go to work for Goodwill was a faith-based desire to use whatever skills I had to benefit others less fortunate. While I did not aspire to be a leader, I did aspire to serve. I have never been interested in having power or control for its own sake, but throughout my adult life I have always been interested in accomplishing something worthwhile and creating something good that would outlast me.

In Houston, the executive training program under Bill Lufburrow could best be described as sink or swim. He was a charismatic visionary, big thinker, and superb orator, frequently described by others as impetuous, impatient, exasperating, exciting, unpredictable, unstoppable, fast moving, and fun. He loved change. I experienced that firsthand when, the first three times I left town after going to work there, I returned to find that my office had been moved. I didn't love change that much, so I quit going away so frequently.

Bill gave me leadership opportunities almost from day one. Shortly after I arrived, he named me sales director. At first, I had no idea what I was doing, but I learned quickly on the job. During the subsequent 16 months, my responsibilities grew. I became part of the leadership team and was exposed to all aspects of the Houston organization. Bill became a valued friend and mentor, and I learned an enormous amount from him.

After that initial 16 months, he sent me to Beaumont, 90 miles from Houston, to run a branch he had started there a few years earlier. It had a lot of problems, and his orders to me were to improve it enough that it could become an independent, autonomous Goodwill within a year. We did it in nine months, during which Bill came over only once and stayed just 15 minutes. I was really on my own.

There can be some definite advantages to assuming the leadership of an organization with a lot of problems. When I arrived in Beaumont, Goodwill there was so bad there was hardly any way I could have failed to improve it. Stores were not open on Sundays in Beaumont in those days, and on Sunday during the weekend I moved there I went to the Goodwill store and washed the windows, which were so filthy you couldn't see through them. I wanted to show improvements and start setting a higher bar from day one.

During my first week on the job, I discovered our truck driver was stealing, so I fired him. As the only person left in the 30-employee organization who had a commercial driver's license, I drove the truck to deliver goods to our store in Port Arthur, 20 miles away. Without the goods our sales would drop, and there was no other way to get them to the store. There was nothing I could have done that day that would have been of more value to the organization. This fell under the part of the job description that read, "Whatever it takes."

There were plenty of other early challenges, and I routinely worked 60-70 hours a week addressing them. Eventually, though, the pluses began to outweigh the minuses. New staff I hired helped us raise the level at which the organization functioned, and we saw a rapidly growing number of positive stories of progress among people with significant disabilities who were looking to us for some help.

In October 1972, we separated from the Houston organization and became an independent community-based Goodwill. I remained there as its CEO for one more year.

Beaumont was where I first realized that I really enjoyed running an organization and making it better. I loved the sense of accomplishment from being able to make things happen that helped improve the lives of people who in many cases hadn't had much of a chance in life. And I found that my values and historic values of Goodwill seemed to align well. Paraphrased, three of those are:

- Every individual has value.

- Work adds meaning and purpose to life, and there is dignity in all useful occupations.

- Goodwill offers opportunity, not charity, and fosters development, not dependency.

Every day, I saw the importance of that second value. A large percentage of the people we employed had seldom, if ever, had any opportunities to work before. They were thrilled to be there. It wasn't just the chance to come to work, earn some money, and feel like they were worthwhile human beings, as important as all of that was. Goodwill was also where they were with other people who often became their friends as well as their coworkers. The break area was usually a place of lively conversation, and there were always a lot more smiles than frowns.

Over time, I developed a strong aversion to the opinions of those who liked to describe some jobs as "menial" and tended to view jobs as "good" or "bad." One size never fits all in such matters. For some of our employees, a job that others might consider beneath them could be the highest type of work they could perform, at least at that time. And, more often than not, they took great pride in doing those jobs as well as possible. It was also gratifying to see some of those individuals learn and grow, develop new skills, and move into different positions – either with us or another employer. All of this reinforced my belief in what we were doing and helped solidify my dedication to the work.

Another reason Goodwill was such a good fit for me was that it gave me the opportunity to exercise entrepreneurial instincts I first started demonstrating when I was eight years old. I never got an allowance and never received any financial reward for making good grades (which I usually did). If I wanted spending money I had to find a way to earn it. More often than not, I succeeded at doing that.

At age eight I sold products such as a salve and Christmas cards that I ordered wholesale from ads in comic books. My customers were compassionate neighbors and relatives. I also mowed lawns. I hated mowing lawns, but I liked the money I made from it.

When I was ten I set up a drive-in theater for bicycles on a vacant lot next to our house. I built a frame out of 2x4s, attached a sheet to it, dug two holes, and "planted" the frame. I bought a 16mm movie projector and some movies – all of them short, silent, black and white cartoons or westerns, ran a long extension cord from the house to my projection stand, and charged the neighborhood kids 10 cents for admission and 10 cents for the popcorn I popped. I kept records of my income and expenses and made a small profit.

When I was 12 I got a newspaper route and kept it for 2-1/2 years. I loved the job! In those days the Lakeland Ledger was an afternoon paper Monday through Friday. It was also published on Sunday mornings. During the week I rode my bicycle (later, my Cushman Eagle motor scooter) to the newspaper office to get my bundle of papers, rolled them, and then delivered them. I timed each part of the job, always trying to beat my record. And I strived to have very satisfied customers, in part because

I hated getting complaints. In addition, though, if they really liked my service they would tip more at Christmas.

I had a variety of other jobs through high school, including painting apartments my grandmother owned, vacuuming the concourse, emptying ash trays, and oiling the lanes before league play at the local bowling alley, and filling out weekly reports at the gas station one of my uncles managed. I also worked for a real estate appraising firm that was doing some work on an urban renewal project in Tampa.

The point of all of this is that running a Goodwill gave me the opportunity to put those same entrepreneurial inclinations to work in ways that helped further the mission of the organization. For someone wired the way I was, it was a wonderful fit.

During the summer of 1973 Alan McNeil, CEO of the Indianapolis-based Goodwill, contacted me. He had become a friend I greatly respected, and he had just learned he had cancer. His number two person had accepted a position as CEO of another Goodwill, and Alan needed help. He asked me to consider joining him as vice president-operations of Goodwill in central Indiana.

Another irony: During the months Goodwill Industries of America was trying to convince me to enter the executive training program, they wanted me to train in Indianapolis. I declined, refusing to consider any place in the Midwest or Northeast. I wanted to live in a warmer climate. But, as I considered Alan's request, I knew that the Indianapolis-based Goodwill was one of the largest and best Goodwills in the country. If I were going to make Goodwill a career, I knew I should seriously consider going there. I also knew I would undoubtedly learn a lot. Long story short: I accepted Alan's offer, resigned my position in Beaumont and moved to Indianapolis. Part of the agreement was that I would stay at least four years. However, if Alan died and someone else was selected to succeed him, I would be released from that commitment.

That was the third multi-year commitment I had made since graduating from Georgia Tech. Subsequently, after a long career building an organization and having many other experiences, I concluded that the greatest accomplishments and life's greatest rewards come from making and keeping long term commitments. I take a long-term view of most things I consider important.

I had a mild form of culture shock when I arrived in Indianapolis. I had enjoyed living in Atlanta when I was a student at Georgia Tech. I loved the way the city's business and civic leaders dreamed big, built big, and made things happen quickly. I saw some of those same characteristics in Houston when I lived there a few years later. Both of those cities were fast moving, rapidly growing, exciting places to be.

By contrast, everything in Indianapolis in the early 1970s seemed to me to move in slow motion. Everything, that is, except the Indy 500. The people were very nice, but many were incredibly cautious and risk averse. It was the only place I had ever lived where I saw more than a few people slow down when approaching *green* lights (Well, you never know, it might change). I began to use that as a metaphor for a lot of what I saw. It also seemed to me that in too many places there was a willingness to accept mediocrity rather than strive for excellence. A common attitude seemed to be, "Well, it's good enough." And for many, change of any kind was resisted as long as possible.

Happily, Indianapolis has grown and changed immensely in the decades since I moved there and has become quite an attractive and often exciting place to live (although now I see some people who don't even stop for *red* lights).

The Indianapolis Goodwill in the early 1970s was also dramatically different from the Houston Goodwill. Bill was a great fit for Houston in those days. He dreamed big and made things happen quickly. His board loved him. Under Alan's leadership, the Indianapolis Goodwill was much more professionally managed, and his board loved the way he ran the organization and fully supported him. To me, though, it seemed slow, bureaucratic, and – dare I say it - boring compared with the Houston Goodwill.

Alan had been with the organization only four years when I arrived there. He was a man of extraordinarily high principles, very bright, kind, thoughtful, and deliberate. He had an accounting background and had instituted a number of processes that made a lot of sense and had been long overdue. He had also launched some significant new initiatives that, sadly, he did not get to see come to fruition. He was a genuinely good person who had become a good friend as well as my boss.

Bill and Alan were very different from each other, but they were also very close friends. And both were very successful Goodwill CEOs. As I was on a steep learning curve and beginning to develop my own leadership style, it was helpful to know that there was more than one way to approach the job. Over time, as my development continued, the style that evolved, while different from either Bill's or Alan's, eventually incorporated elements of each of theirs. I definitely benefited from having worked under two successful CEOs who had dramatically different styles.

Unfortunately, seven months after I arrived in Indianapolis Alan died at the age of 36. The board named me Acting Director and two months later made me President and CEO of Goodwill Industries of Central Indiana. I was 30 years old.

# CHAPTER 2

## *Early Leadership Experiences*

Throughout my adult life the more I learn, the more I realize how little I know. But in the early years of my career, I had no idea how much I needed to learn.

One day I was standing in our workshop in Beaumont staring off into space, thinking about some layout changes I wanted to make. Suddenly, I was aware that one of the workers on a conveyor belt at least 20 feet away had left her position and was standing directly in front of me, looking very worried. She asked, "Am I doing something wrong?" I quickly realized that I had been staring in her direction, and I knew she had a history of mental illness. She had assumed if I was staring at her, she must have been doing something wrong. I tried to never make that mistake again.

In Indianapolis, even though I had been in a senior position with the organization for nine months, the way I was perceived by others in the organization suddenly changed when I became CEO. I didn't view myself any differently. But I quickly learned that simply by being in the CEO position, many others viewed me differently than before and differently from how I viewed myself. They were watching me and could draw all sorts of conclusions just from the expression on my face or the tone of my voice.

I could ruin a person's day if I happened to be preoccupied and failed to say hello to someone I had passed in the hall. They would assume I was mad at them and wonder why. I also learned that I couldn't think out loud and had to be careful with what I said, even in passing. One day I made a casual remark that someday we needed to paint the hall. Someone walking by overheard the remark, and the next day the hall was painted. While I appreciated the fact that the hall looked a lot better, I hadn't intended for those who painted it to put other projects on hold because they assumed I wanted the hall painted right away. I needed to be more careful with what I said and, when I did want something done, to make sure others knew where it fit among various priorities.

Later, the opposite happened. I had a lot of ideas. But if I sent too many of those ideas out too quickly, nothing happened. I finally realized I was asking them to do more than was possible; they didn't know which to do and which not to do, so they did none of them. I had to learn to pace the flow of ideas for improvement I'd toss out.

Those were some of the early learnings of a very young, inexperienced executive. I later thought that if, when I became CEO of the Indianapolis Goodwill I had any idea how little I knew at the time, I would have been scared to death. But I had a lot of confidence, warranted or not; I was eager to learn and eager to make things happen. In stark contrast with what I found when I moved to Beaumont, Goodwill in Indianapolis was a well-run, respected organization with a sound financial position. Still, there's always a lot of room for improvement in any organization, and from my perspective that was certainly the case at Goodwill in Indianapolis. I moved quickly, made a lot of changes, and ruffled a lot of feathers along the way – in some cases unnecessarily so. That was especially true when, in my haste to make things happen, I didn't take enough time to explain why I thought the changes were needed and to get those who would be affected on board. And my learning process accelerated.

Throughout my career I read an enormous number of books and articles about leadership, management, and organizations. I learned more from the writings of Peter Drucker, arguably the premier thinker and writer on those topics during the second half of the 20th Century, than any other author. I had early exposure to Drucker in an introductory industrial management course I took at Georgia Tech that used his book, *The Practice of Management*, for a text. I loved the examples he used that helped me see different ways to define the purpose of a business or approach a problem.

I also began attending workshops, seminars, and conferences where I thought I might learn something that would help me do my job better. And I began visiting other Goodwills that were outperforming us in certain areas to see what I could learn from them. Later, I was just as interested in learning what I could from outside the "Goodwill family." Gary Hamel wrote that "most people in an industry are blind in the same way; they're all paying attention to the same things and not paying attention to the same things." We tried not to fall into that trap.

Some other notes from Hamel (*Leading the Revolution*, Harvard Business School Press, 2000):

- *Insights come from new conversations. All too often, strategy conversations in large companies have the same ten people talking to the same ten people for the fifth year in a row. They can finish each other's sentences. You're not going to learn anything new in this setting.*

- *There is so much individuals cannot imagine simply because they are prisoners of their own dogma.*

- *The more you pay attention to information that supports your world view the less you learn.*

- *You can't use an old map to find a new land.*

I also benefited tremendously from having a board that saw potential in me and was willing to give me time to grow into the job. Without my knowing it, a small group of the board agreed among themselves to "form a cocoon around me" to mentor me, support me, and keep me from making any big mistakes. I am forever grateful to them.

Despite this desire of the board to help me learn and grow, during my first several years I was too hesitant to ask for help or seek advice from others. I was trying to be too independent and could have benefited a lot from more good coaching. Eventually, I recognized and corrected this flaw and in the years since have seldom refused to try to help others who have asked me to serve as a mentor for them.

But I also had to learn how to work well with the board. The first time I brought to the board a proposal to implement a new program – a different approach to the way we helped people get jobs with other firms, I was momentarily stunned at the first question that was asked. A longtime member of the board who was president of a large retailer in Indianapolis asked, "Is anyone else doing this?" The inference as I took it was that if no other Goodwills were doing it, why should we? Shouldn't we wait until the concept was proven elsewhere? The question seemed to me to reflect the risk-averse attitude very common in Indiana in those days.

I hesitated a few seconds and then replied, "I don't know, but I think we should try it." The board member who had asked the question then said, "Oh, OK. Go ahead and try it." To me, that was a breakthrough. I don't remember much about the program itself, but it was at least modestly successful. And it helped me establish a pattern of trying things whether any other Goodwill had done them before or not.

In the early decades of my career, strategic planning in many organizations was a discrete event that was performed every 3-5 years. It typically resulted in a thick document, much of which wasn't very useful after the first year or two. Because I didn't know any better, we followed that pattern for a long time, starting in 1976.

During the last 10-15 years of my career, though, strategic planning in our organization morphed into more of a continuous strategic *thinking* process. In part, this was a response to how quickly our external environment was changing and how much we were learning. Instead of having a thick strategic plan, we began to use a much slimmer document titled

Strategic Directions that was updated annually. In a world that seemed to be increasingly complex, with greater uncertainty and ambiguity in so much of what we encountered, this proved to be far more useful.

While our leadership team and a committee or task group of the board were always heavily involved, throughout my career I led the strategic planning processes. I tend to be a systems thinker and enjoyed putting what we were doing or might do into a larger context and seeing how we could fit the pieces together. In addition, during the latter part of my career, with others handling day-to-day matters quite well, I was able to spend much more of my time on long range and strategic issues and new initiatives.

The board's involvement in the planning process was significant, though. They asked hard questions that forced us to really think through what we were proposing, and they made a lot of suggestions. Ultimately, the final document required board approval. This process worked well for us.

Over the next four decades, several aspects of my makeup became obvious to those who followed what we did at Goodwill:

- I have never been content with the status quo and have always had a drive to improve whatever I'm involved with. If I ever started feeling too comfortable with how we were doing at Goodwill, the mere awareness of that feeling made me uncomfortable. One day I mentioned this to a friend who told me, "In India they have a term for that: it's called divine discontent." Personally, I never thought of it as in any way divine. To me, it was more of a curse.

- I'm also generally comfortable challenging conventional wisdom and systems and structures that don't make sense to me. Some of my biggest frustrations arose from the gap between what was and what could be, and I was constantly trying to close that gap. At times my impatience was a detriment. However, I tried hard not to let the perfect be the enemy of the good.

- I tend to be pragmatic and am primarily interested in what works, as long as it doesn't conflict with my values.

- I'm a generalist with a lot of interests. I do not consider myself an expert in anything. But, where we needed experts I hired them, and a big part of our success resulted from my hiring people who could do their jobs far better than I could have done them.

During those four decades we tried many ways to grow our businesses and accomplish our mission. We learned from all our experiences and from the experiences of others. Along the way, we adapted reasonably well most of the time to the enormous changes taking place in the world we operated in. And as we tried things, learned, and adapted, we evolved as an organization.

Many of those experiences constitute the next two parts of this book.

# PART II

*Trying Things, Learning, Adapting*

# FOOD FOR THOUGHT

## Newton's Laws and Organizations

*In high school and college physics, I became well acquainted with Sir Isaac Newton's Laws of Motion. Over time, I've seen many ways in which the concepts underlying at least two of those three laws apply to organizations as well as to the physical world.*

*For example, Newton's First Law of Motion - the Law of Inertia - is often paraphrased as "A body at rest will stay at rest until acted upon by an external force." How can that apply to organizations? One way I've observed is that the more an organization is removed from day-to-day competition (a powerful external force), the slower it tends to be to adapt as its external environment changes.*

*When you are subject to competition on a day-to-day basis, there's more of a sense of urgency, more of a drive to improve. You know that if you don't improve, someone is going to take your customers (or clients, students, patients) away from you. For organizations that lack strong competition, the faster the rate of change on the outside, the more they tend to lag. They might survive, but they are likely to become increasingly ineffective or irrelevant.*

*To excel in the absence of external forces such as strong competition, an organization needs highly effective leadership – a strong internal force. Those who provide such leadership have high standards, set challenging goals, and lead in a way that helps others in their organizations perform at a high level. And they are never satisfied with the status quo.*

*Surviving, but becoming increasingly ineffective or irrelevant, is generally not as much of a problem in the for-profit world as it can be in the public and not-for-profit sectors. In the for-profit world, if you don't successfully adapt to external changes - including new or stronger competition - in most cases you will eventually become extinct. Ineffective or irrelevant not-for-profits also can and sometimes do become extinct, but depending on their sources of income, some of them might survive far longer than would be warranted by their mission-related impact.*

*Newton's Third Law of Motion - or a reasonable facsimile thereof - also applies to institutions. This law is often stated, "For every action there is an equal and opposite reaction." A Corollary might go something like this: "For every excess there will be a proportionate reaction and correction. The greater the excess, the greater the pain associated with the correction."*

*Examples abound! Excessive spending by individuals, organizations, or governments will eventually prompt a correction. Sometimes the correction will come only after years of excess. But eventually it will come. And with the correction will come pain proportionate to the degree of excess.*

*Of course, excessive conservatism can also be a problem. Companies that do not spend enough to properly maintain their physical assets, retain and develop their people, and improve their productivity are jeopardizing their future. They can also jeopardize their future when they fail to invest in opportunities for which they are well-suited, thus leaving the door open for more aggressive, well-managed competitors to increase their strength.*

*Governments - cities, states, nations - that fail to adequately maintain their infrastructures will eventually have a huge price to pay - and you can count on a strong reaction from their citizens when the bill and the pain associated with it come due. The same applies to those public sector entities that fail to adequately fund their future obligations (e.g., pension systems).*

*I suggest that societies that don't invest enough to prevent problems and help kids develop – especially those kids at higher risk and whose families have limited resources – eventually pay much more downstream for remediation, rehabilitation, incarceration, and in all the ways we all pay when we don't have a workforce with adequate skills for the times.*

*Of course, the dilemma we all face is how to know how far we can go in either direction (too much or too little) before it's excessive enough to prompt a strong reaction or overreaction, which will then prompt another correction. Unfortunately, there's no magic answer. It's a judgment call, and we seldom have all the information we wish we had when we need to make big decisions. Perhaps this is one reason why progress is rarely, if ever, linear.*

# CHAPTER 3

## A World of Change

I was CEO of Goodwill in Indiana so long that, a few years before I retired, a member of our board who was a CPA jokingly described me as a fixed asset, fully depreciated. At least he didn't consider me a liability!

During those four decades the world around us changed in phenomenal ways. I'm grateful I never had to face a pandemic during my career, but we did have to adapt to enormous changes in demographics, the economy, competition, laws, and regulations. We encountered six recessions, adapted to 15 increases in the federal minimum wage, and were affected by several geopolitical events. We also had to adapt to a wide range of gradual sociological and cultural changes in the U.S. during those decades.

Some of the biggest changes were technological. When I started working for Goodwill I was still using a slide rule at times. Our first computer was an IBM System 3, a big box that had far less computer power than a smart phone today and that we used solely for accounting functions.

In the early 1970s we repaired a lot of radios and TVs that had been donated to Goodwill by replacing bad vacuum tubes. Simple. Solid state electronics eliminated that.

Another example: Shortly before I arrived in Indianapolis, Goodwill had secured a contract with the U.S. General Services Administration to manufacture wooden file boxes for 3x5 and 5x8 index cards. My predecessor had taken the initiative to obtain the contract under the provisions of the 1971 Javits-Wagner-O'Day Act (JWOD – later to be known as the

AbilityOne program), which used federal procurement to boost employment of people with significant disabilities. Goodwill had never manufactured wood products, but prior to my arrival had ordered the equipment that would be needed. However, no one in the organization knew how to make a file box. So we hired a supervisor with a lot of relevant experience and became quite proficient at it. Eighteen of our employees, at least 75% of whom had significant disabilities, produced a total of more than 50,000 boxes a year, and the operation was profitable for 18 years. Eventually, though, the government's growing use of computers reduced and finally eliminated the need for our file boxes. A new technology rendered our product obsolete.

The capabilities we had developed to make file boxes had proven useful in another way, though. In 1987 we were asked to make 4,000 "spine boards" (wooden stretchers) for the U.S. Defense Department. It was a one-time order and we expected to receive no more. Then, in January 1991, the Defense Department sent us an order for 5,000 spine boards and wanted them in two weeks. The next week, the first Gulf War started. We manufactured the boards and shipped them shortly after that mercifully brief war ended.

While we terminated all our wood products operations in 1992, in March 2003 we received a call from a government official who wanted to know if we could make 5,000 spine boards to be delivered in one week. We had to decline, as we were no longer in that business. The War on Iraq started two weeks after we received the call.

Wood products manufacturing was a profitable mission-enhancing venture that employed a significant number of people with disabilities for a significant number of years. It was a home run, but not one of the few I consider a grand slam.

New technologies eliminated some jobs in our organization but created others. When I retired in 2015 our e-commerce unit employed over 100 people and our internal IT Department employed 25. One of those was Andy, a young man who came to us as a 9th grade student in the first high school we opened. He had had a rough home life, but he thrived in our school. We employed him part-time while he was in college, and after graduating he worked full-time in our IT Department. Andy was the person who was usually assigned to help me with technology issues in my office. I appreciated his patience with me as well as his skill. After working for Goodwill for a few years Andy accepted an offer to work in IT at a large company headquartered in Indianapolis.

Another of our IT employees came to us as a new Syrian immigrant with no tangible assets, but a strong desire to learn and earn his own way. He started out in an entry level retail position in one of our stores and within a very few years was promoted to a professional position in IT.

Problems in the Middle East had affected us far earlier, though, than the situation that resulted in our Syrian friend's connection with our organization. Goodwill has always received a lot of donations of clothing that is not good enough to be placed in our stores, and some of what *is* good enough doesn't sell. Fortunately, there has long been a good secondary market for such items, which typically are sold in large bales to third parties that export it. Much of it winds up in less developed countries.

The textile salvage market is affected by currency fluctuations and, at times, by geopolitical events. Such was the case in 1976, when much of what we were selling to brokers was being shipped through Beirut. When the civil war in Lebanon started, the port was bombed, and the textile salvage market was almost completely halted for several months until other distribution channels could be developed. The result for Goodwill in Indianapolis and many other organizations was an inability to sell our textile salvage at any price.

We responded by purchasing several cutting machines and going into the wiping cloth business. We cut up as much as we could and sold it locally to auto garages and others who needed a lot of rags. That created jobs for 14 people with disabilities and was profitable for several years. We ended the operation after the textile salvage market had once again become strong and the market for wiping cloths such as those we made was declining due to the development of lower cost alternatives.

Changes in public policy could present us with new opportunities or prompt changes in some of what we were already doing. For example, shortly after I became CEO, an initiative begun under my predecessor needed action. There was a rapidly growing movement nationally to move people in large institutions such as state hospitals into small community-based facilities. Federal public policy strongly encouraged and was quite supportive of this "deinstitutionalization" movement, and we had an opportunity to become part of it. While I had no in-depth knowledge of the topic, the concept sounded good and our board was supportive. So with a lot of help from the Indianapolis Community Service Council, we applied for and received a "national demonstration grant" from the U.S. Department of Health, Education, and Welfare to establish and operate a group home – the first of its kind in Indianapolis - for people with developmental disabilities – many of them individuals with epilepsy - who were to be moved out of the New Castle State Hospital. Goodwill would provide the residents with vocational training and employment services as well as life skills training and a place to live.

We found a suitable property with two buildings on it, bought it with funds from the Goodwill Foundation, remodeled the buildings, and operated the program successfully for twelve years. By 1987, though, government regulations and funding mechanisms for such programs had become much more complex, and we concluded that we needed to be in that business in a big way or not at all. In those days we did not have the depth or breadth of talent to create a large residential services component and still maintain the level of vocational services we had developed, and we decided that our primary focus should remain on vocational services. We then sold the residential facility to a for-profit operator of group homes. More than 40 years later, those buildings were still being used as a group home.

Of course, we frequently had to adapt to changing economic conditions – none in my career more difficult than what we faced during a deep recession in the early 1980s. Statewide unemployment in Indiana rose from 6.4% in 1979 to 10.1% in 1981 and peaked at 11.9% in 1982. It did not drop below 11% until 1984. Goodwill operated vocational training programs in upholstery, micrographics, electronics assembly, offset printing, data entry and word processing, document encoding, cafeteria/food service, and custodial work. Nearly all those programs were at capacity, but there were few jobs for those who completed training.

Goodwill's internal work base was also shrinking, in part because of the recession. During the first decade of my career, the largest customer of our Industrial Services Division (later renamed the Commercial Services Division) was Western Electric, which manufactured telephones at a plant in Indianapolis. Western Electric was part of the AT&T system, which at that time was regulated by the federal government. Among other jobs, we packaged telephone buttons and installed return springs. The work was dependable, and the margins were good. Then the telephone industry was deregulated and, in a consent decree, AT&T was broken up. The Western Electric plant in Indianapolis became a casualty, and our contract with them ended in 1984.

Other customers in the 1970s and early 1980s included GM's Guide Division in Anderson (we spray painted oil caps and hood ornaments for Oldsmobiles), Union Carbide (we manufactured wiring harnesses), Bryant Heating and Air Conditioning, and Von Duprin. However, our customers - most of whom were durable goods manufacturers - were hit by the recession, and Goodwill's volume of business was directly affected.

Goodwill's retail business was also hurt by the recession. Some people think that retail operations such as Goodwill's should thrive during tough economic times. But if people aren't buying new goods, they're not donating their used goods. Since sales in a Goodwill store are significantly dependent on the quantity and quality of donations, when donations drop, so do sales.

I decided that if no one else would hire the people we were training that we would start businesses and employ them ourselves. We also knew we had to do something different just to be able to continue employing everyone already on our payroll, and many of them were the primary source of income in their households.

Over the next several years we were very entrepreneurial.

- In 1983 we bought franchises in a home cleaning business. The venture started out strong but hit a plateau from which we were never able to budge. We also learned the hard way that homeowners willing to pay what we had to charge were very picky. We didn't do a good enough job consistently enough, and the entire effort required far too much attention from upper management. We finally ended our relationship with the parent company in 1988.

- Also in 1983, we bought the assets of a small California company that had been manufacturing fabric cases for cassette tapes. We had learned about them from a Minneapolis-based record distributing company that had a large distribution center in Indianapolis for which we processed unsold records. They told us if we made the fabric cases, they would buy them from us. We paid $10,000 for the equipment and patterns, moved the equipment to Indianapolis, started manufacturing the cases, and hired a company to market them for us. We never sold any of them – not even to the company that had promised to buy them. The product was simply not price-competitive with plastic cases coming from Asia.

- In 1984 we established an industrial sewing unit and began manufacturing scrubs and lab coats for the local market. We started off strong, but eventually found we could not compete on price with companies that had similar products made in Asia. Thus, our sales volume was too low for the business to be financially sustainable.

- Also in 1984, we started a business to refinish institutional furniture. We got the idea from a large workshop in upstate New York. Our customers included universities (mostly dormitory furniture), hotels, and restaurants. We tried to get the state hospital business but could not compete on price with Prison Industries. We did good work, but after three or four years our volume reached a plateau, while costs continued increasing dramatically because of tighter regulations on the disposal of hazardous waste. Rather than make major new investments and continue to incur increased liability exposure, we shut the operation down in 1989.

By the mid-1980s, without realizing what we were doing, we had created a mini conglomerate of small businesses. (Note: You do not want to do this.) While a few of them never got traction, others quickly reached a plateau at $200-250,000 a year. We didn't have the capital to grow any of them, and what management talent we had in those days was spread so thin I'm not sure we did anything as well as we should have. Fortunately, we had not invested much money in any of those ventures, and our losses weren't large. As the economy improved and jobs became more plentiful, we eventually shut down all those little businesses.

On the plus side, we were able to keep most of our people working during a period of very high unemployment, with the overall impact of those little ventures helping at the margins. And we had certainly learned a lot about how hard it is to start and operate small businesses. We had also learned a lot about the hazards of over-diversifying. I later categorized some of those little ventures as singles, but the overall strategy was a strikeout.

While we learned some important lessons from those experiences, I knew I needed to learn a lot more to be an effective executive, and I enrolled in the two-year Executive MBA program offered at that time by what is now the Kelley School of Business at Indiana University. I went through with a cohort of 30 people, most of whom were in middle management positions in large companies. I was the only one who worked in a not-for-profit. We got to know each other pretty well, and as we compared experiences I was surprised to learn that some of those big companies were doing even dumber things than we were. It seemed that most of our problems were similar in nature and had to do with people. And while I learned a lot from my coursework, I also learned a lot from my classmates and concluded that at Goodwill we were better than I had thought, but not nearly as good as we could be. It was a great learning experience and confidence booster for me.

In 1986, the year I completed my MBA, we obtained our first federal service contract under the provisions of AbilityOne. Service contracts under AbilityOne provide stable jobs with good wages and good working conditions and, if managed well, generate reasonable margins. At least 75% of the direct labor hours must be provided by people with significant disabilities. Once a qualified not-for-profit organization secures a contract under AbilityOne, the relevant product or service is removed from the competitive bidding process. Thus, an organization can continue to provide that product or service as long as it meets the requirements of the contract and the government continues to need that product or service.

Our first contract was to provide shelf stocking and janitorial services in the Commissary at what was then Ft. Benjamin Harrison. We still had that contract when I retired 29 years later.

We subsequently added 10 more AbilityOne contracts that collectively employed 223 people in 2015. The lowest starting wage was $11/hour plus a benefit package worth more than $3.00/hour. Goodwill employees on those contracts cleaned 2.5 million square feet of space a day and provided grounds keeping and mailroom services, in addition to the shelf stocking services in the Commissary.

We had to meet all the requirements that any other firm doing the same work would have to meet, and our people consistently performed at a very high level.

For our organization and the people we served, those contracts were a true grand slam. They benefited a lot of people; they lasted a long time; and they were financially sustainable.

From a national perspective, the AbilityOne program could be used more extensively to provide work at good wages and benefits for people who are frequently among the last to be hired and the first to be laid off by many companies. Those contracts work well for the workers, the federal government, and for society.

While the AbilityOne program has its critics, when all factors are included, using this program to employ people who otherwise might not be working is far less expensive than would be the combined cost of providing entitlements and other income supports to those individuals while also paying another contractor to provide the services that could have been performed under an AbilityOne contract.

Add the intangible value of this program to the employees and members of their families, and the total benefits to society are enormous.

Throughout my career, we worked hard to maintain good relationships with units of state and local government, regardless of which party was in power. With a mission that had a lot of appeal to liberals and conservatives alike, and in a period in our nation's history when politics was much less polarized than it later became, we were nearly always able to do that. Of course, there were many changes over the years in laws and regulations. From our perspective, some of those were helpful, others not so much. But we usually managed to adapt without compromising our values or our mission.

There was one situation, though, where a change in political leadership and subsequent changes in contract management by a new political appointee led to a situation where we could not meet the terms of the contract and still adhere to a level of service that we could be proud of. Eventually, this led to the contracting agency terminating the contract we had to operate the one-stop employment service centers in Indianapolis.

In those centers we had contact with approximately 50,000 unemployed people each year. Of those, between 8,000 and 12,000 eventually became employed. However, the contracts under which the centers were operated were highly prescriptive; many of those who used them were primarily looking for unemployment checks; and a significant percentage of those who did become employed were not able to keep the jobs and came back through the system two or, in some cases, three times a year.

We began to question whether we even wanted to continue our involvement, as it was increasingly apparent that the level of service we were able to provide was below our normal standards. In addition, the contract performance requirements made it very difficult for us to assist individuals with more serious problems. The more we did that, the greater the difficulty we had meeting the performance targets specified in the contracts. Eventually, after we missed one of the targets, the person who ran the local contracting agency – a person appointed following a change in political leadership after we already had the contract - took advantage of the opportunity to "fire" us. I was angry at having our contract terminated for non-performance, but it turned out to be a blessing in disguise. We established new criteria for entering into contracts with public sector entities and made sure we were always in a position to provide quality services that had high potential for lasting impact.

The experience operating those centers had one other major positive effect. Some of what we learned through it factored into changes that eventually led to a transformation of our services, a rapid increase in the evolution of the entire organization, and a quantum leap in lasting impact. More on that in Chapter 12.

# FOOD FOR THOUGHT

## *On Change*

*A*t Goodwill, we had the good fortune to be subject to day-to-day market forces in the largest part of the organization. Unfortunately, the more an organization is removed from such forces, the greater the danger it will develop tunnel vision and eventually be blindsided. In addition, in some not-for-profits, some of those in leadership positions can be so focused on and passionate about what they are doing that they don't recognize external threats quickly enough.

Regardless of how much you are affected by market forces, though, change is usually difficult. In our organization, change was normal and expected, though certainly not always loved and embraced. We managed most major changes reasonably well, but at other times we could have done a much better job planning, executing the changes, and communicating with those who would be affected. While we always tried to minimize the impact of significant changes on our people, I eventually concluded that the more we can help our employees learn and grow, the better able they will be to adapt to the changes they will face – in our organization, with other employers, or in other aspects of their lives.

Continuous learning, in fact, might be one of the keys to effectively adapting in an era of rapid change. As Eric Hoffer wrote, "In a time of drastic change it is the learners who inherit the future, while the learned usually find themselves beautifully equipped to live in a world that no longer exists."

<u>*Some of my favorite quotes on the subject of change*</u>

*It is not necessary to change. Survival is not mandatory.*

*J. Edwards Deming*

*Change is not a problem to be overcome. It is the essence of business success*

*From <u>Complexity and the Nexus of Leadership</u>*
*By Goldstein, Hazy, and Liechtenstein*

*Change is debilitating when done to us but exhilarating when done by us.*

*Rosabeth Moss Kantor*

*People don't resist change. They resist <u>being</u> changed.*

*Richard Teerlink*

*No organization is so screwed up somebody doesn't like it as it is.*

*Anonymous*

*He stayed the same as before, but the same was no longer befitting.*

*Cicero*

*Change is good. You go first.*

*Dilbert*

*If you can't learn to love change, at least learn to live with it without whining too much.*

*Jim McClelland (I had to include one of my own.)*

# CHAPTER 4

## *Building a Team*

A major turning point for our organization and for me personally took place in April 1987 when I woke up one beautiful spring morning having a heart attack. I was 43 years old.

I had been well aware that the men in my family for the previous two generations had died relatively young, nearly always from cardiovascular problems. And I had high cholesterol that we had been treating with the medications that were then available. I had also been very disciplined about diet and exercise. In fact, I had been a runner for 20 years. But the genes had more influence.

At Goodwill, the staff did well during my absence, but while I was recovering I resolved to build a team that would be so strong they could run the organization successfully for six months or more in case I died or was otherwise unable to function. Over the next few years that decision had an enormously positive impact on the growth in size, strength, and impact of the organization.

Even before the heart attack I had begun trying to attract better talent to fill positions that reported directly to me. I found that if I paid a little more, we got a lot more. The brighter, more talented people would earn their keep many times over. Of course, from time to time we also had people in key positions who were not able to grow sufficiently as the organization was growing. Inevitably, they had to be replaced.

One of the most difficult decisions I had to make during the first few years of my career involved a widely revered man who ran what in those days we referred to as our Rehabilitation Division. He had been with Goodwill for over 30 years, starting as a "client" in a rehabilitation program and rising to become vice president of one of the most important parts of our organization. Dedicated and compassionate, he was a superb human being who used a wheelchair because of quadriplegia. Since my arrival, I had left that division totally in his hands.

When I began to pay more attention to that part of the organization, though, I became concerned that we were not continuing to develop the way we should, and the excellent reputation I knew that division had enjoyed through the 1960s had diminished. I asked a consultant from Goodwill's national office to come in and take a look at what we were doing. After a couple of days looking at our programs and talking with our people, he came to me and said, "Jim, this was a really good program – 20 years ago." It was stuck in a time warp and needed new leadership.

I agonized over what to do. Finally, I came up with the idea of creating a new position for that vice president that would allow him to continue to have a significant role at Goodwill, but that would remove him from any operational responsibilities. When I discussed it with him, though, he was offended and decided to retire. We gave him a nice sendoff, but I never felt I handled that situation as well as I might have.

The best decisions I made in my entire career were good hiring decisions. Conversely, of course, the worst decisions I made were bad hiring decisions. Fortunately, most of those happened relatively early in my career. My batting average improved significantly when I began to include other members of our leadership team in the process when we were seeking to fill a high-level position. While I always made the final decision, I strongly considered the opinions of other members of our team – for skills, yes, but also for "fit" with our culture.

On two occasions Goodwill achieved what I viewed as a critical mass of talent. The first, which primarily involved my direct reports, occurred around 1995 and was followed by an increased rate of growth. The second, which occurred around 2005, was in depth as well as breadth and prompted even more rapid growth in size and impact. In our donated goods/retail, commercial services, and support functions, most of our leaders, managers, supervisors, and professional staff came to us from for-profit backgrounds, including some from Fortune 500 companies. In our schools, other direct human services, and fund raising areas, most of our people came to us from not-for-profits or public sector entities. In our culture, the mix generally worked well.

One of my best decisions in the 1980s was to hire George Galyean, who from the mid-1980s till 2005 led the growth and development of our donated goods/retail operations – the financial backbone of the entire organization. George had a business background and had come to us from a manufacturing company headquartered in Indianapolis. Initially, he led our Industrial Services Division, but I soon asked him to head up our donated goods/retail operations as well. He also hired Kent Kramer to continue building and improving our retail division in subsequent years. In 2015 Kent succeeded me as President and CEO.

Following my heart attack I began seeking people who could run other parts of the organization at a much higher level, and the stronger the team became, the more I delegated to them. They handled day-to-day operations better than I could have, enabling me to spend more of my time on long range and strategic matters and new initiatives.

Even then, though, I focused my attention primarily on the revenue generating areas and benignly neglected the support functions. Eventually, I began to recognize that if the support services were able to perform at a higher level, they could significantly help the revenue generating areas improve their performance. Dan Riley greatly improved the Accounting Department (and, later, several other areas as well), and Cindy Graham took the Marketing Department to a new level. Human Resources, though, remained an area that left a lot to be desired. The department was viewed as a necessary evil, heavily compliance oriented, and not an area our operations people considered an asset to them.

With input from some friends in the community who knew a lot more about HR than I did, I became convinced that with the right leadership that department could become a valued asset. The result of that overdue realization was the hiring of Keith Reissaus in 1998. Because the department had such a bad reputation internally, we rebranded it Employee and Organization Development (EOD), and Keith went to work changing every aspect of it. He recruited a strong team under him, and over time they in turn helped recruit a lot of terrifically talented people for all parts of the organization. Within a few years EOD became one of our strongest support functions, and it continued to be so under Zaida Monell after Keith retired.

Not long after Keith arrived, he recommended we build our culture around the Five Basic Principles we had articulated a few years earlier in a Total Quality Management seminar participated in by 57 of our staff. We decided to do so, and that turned out to be a major step in the development of the culture we had for the rest of my career. I elaborate on this in the next chapter.

With the enormously positive impact our improved support functions had on the overall performance of our organization, I concluded that a lot of not-for-profit organizations make a great mistake by trying to minimize overhead. The objective should be to optimize it. At our size when I retired ($130M+/year) and level of complexity (high) and with a wealth of superb talent, our general and administrative expenses, which I considered to be close to optimal, totaled 11% of our operating revenue.

# FOOD FOR THOUGHT

## Some Basics for Developing a High

## Performing Organization

- *Understand the goal. Know what you want to accomplish, how it fits into a larger context, and how you will measure success.*

- *Put people in positions where they will be able to use their abilities and perform at a high level. Make sure they have the tools, other resources, environment, and an organizational culture that will enhance their performance.*

  - *It's the leader's job to make resources productive. This applies regardless of the leader's title (e.g., CEO, director, manager, supervisor, coach, principal, superintendent, etc.). Every person and every organization will have strengths and weaknesses. Organize around and build on the strengths; make the weaknesses irrelevant. Never put a person in a position where a weakness of that individual would undermine prospects for success. Never set a person up to fail.*

  - *The leader should provide support, encouragement, coaching, feedback, constructive criticism when necessary, and should help each person continue to learn, grow, and develop. The leader might also need to help resolve problems and conflicts that arise, as well as know when to stay out of the way and let people learn and grow from their experiences.*

- *Crucial questions: Can the leader attract and keep talented people? Do talented people want to work for this person? Does this person help good people become even better?*

- *As much as possible, people should seek positions where:*

  - *There is a good values fit.*

  - *They can use their abilities to a substantial degree.*

  - *They can learn and grow.*

  - *They are likely to enjoy the people they work with.*

  *To what extent does the leader provide such opportunities?*

- *Align everything in the organization toward accomplishment of the goal(s) and do everything possible to ensure that the organization's internal bureaucracy functions as an enabler and not a hindrance to accomplishing the primary goals.*


*Finally, as Collins and Porras emphasized in their book, <u>Built to Last - Successful Habits of Visionary Companies</u> (HarperBusiness, 1994), remember that organizations that thrive, not merely survive over long periods of time have constancy of purpose and a few core values. But everything else changes over time as new needs and opportunities arise and as the external environment changes.*

# CHAPTER 5

## *Corporate Culture*

As I mentioned in the introduction, when I retired as Goodwill's CEO in 2015, the diverse array of operations at Goodwill in central Indiana included:

- 59 retail stores

- e-commerce and recycling operations

- 12 public charter high schools with a total of 3,500 students

- A contract packaging and small assembly division

- Ten commercial services sites

- A home visitation program for 600 first-time mothers in low-income households

Our stores had four million customer transactions and two million donor transactions per year. We cleaned 2.5 million sq. ft. of space for the federal government, and our schools provided high school education opportunities for students ranging in age from 14 to over 60.

Eleven of the schools were Excel Centers, diploma-granting schools designed for older youth and adults who lacked high school diplomas. The demographics of those schools varied enormously depending on their location. Some were predominantly white; others were predominantly black. One of the schools had students representing 23 nationalities and nine native languages – including Tongan and Bantu – other than English. In another school, Spanish was the first language of 40% of the students.

Our organization had a total of 3,300 employees. Two-thirds of them had limited vocational options because of one or more barriers such a significant disability (37%), felony conviction (12%), or lack of a high school diploma (34%). Our staff included licensed teachers, 34 registered nurses, CPAs, MBAs, engineers, and two lawyers. Four percent of our 3,300 employees had post-graduate degrees.

This amazingly diverse array of people was scattered over 80+ locations in central Indiana – from small towns and rural areas to the Indianapolis metropolitan area with a population of two million.

How did we manage an organization with that degree of diversity?

A number of thought leaders have written that culture trumps strategy. For example, in a 2011 article titled "The Global Innovation 1000: Why Culture is Key," published by Booz & Company, authors Barry Jaruzelski, John Loehr, and Richard Holman wrote, "Studies have shown again and again that there may be no more critical source of business success or failure than a company's culture. That isn't to say that strategy doesn't matter, but rather that the particular strategy a company employs will succeed only if it is supported by the appropriate cultural attributes."

A corporate culture is defined largely by:

- Who you hire and retain and the way and extent to which you help your people develop

- What you recognize and reward

- How the leaders act

- How you allocate resources

Organizations that want to perform at a high level over a relatively long period of time need a culture based on a set of articulated values that, when exemplified in the way people go about their work, result in the desired performance. The culture must be one in which people understand that while achieving the business goals is important, how you achieve them is equally important.

In our organization, the operating cultures of different areas varied considerably. For example, the operating culture in a retail store is very different from that of a high school for adults, which is very different from that of a high school for a high-poverty, high-special-needs population of teen-age students. But while the operating cultures varied, all parts of the organization had to observe certain values and basic principles. Those included some historic values of Goodwill Industries:

- Every individual has value.

- Work adds meaning and purpose to life, and there is dignity in all useful occupations.

- Goodwill provides opportunity, not charity, and fosters development, not dependency.

In addition, as noted in the previous chapter, we ingrained in our culture the Five Basic Principles that applied at all levels in all parts of the organization. Those five principles were:

- Respect for people – We strive to treat everyone in a respectful manner.

- Customer Satisfaction – We strive to meet or exceed the expectations customers, donors, and users of our services have of us.

- Innovation and Improvement – We continuously seek better ways to grow, improve, and increase our impact.

- Informed decision-making – We gather relevant information and, to the extent possible, make decisions based on facts.

- Good stewardship – We are responsible stewards of all our resources.

Those principles were built into our recruitment and hiring, onboarding, and performance development review processes, and our people at all levels took them very seriously. The respect principle was particularly important. Depending on the seriousness of the incident, someone who violated it might get a second chance, but would probably not get a third.

We found it was a lot easier and more effective to manage according to a small number of values and basic principles than a thick book of rules and regulations. We had to have some of those, of course, but we tried to keep them to a minimum.

One of the keys to the success of our organization over a relatively long period of time was our ability to attract and keep a lot of terrifically talented people. As a relatively large, diversified organization, much of which operated in a highly competitive environment, we required a level of talent comparable to that of any organization of similar size and complexity in any of the sectors. Fortunately, we were able to attract and keep a lot of people who consistently performed at that level.

What was the key? We didn't really have any "secret sauce." Perhaps it was different for different people, and perhaps it was the sum of several elements that reflected our culture. Those included:

- A mission and a variety of services that were easy to become passionate about. There was generally a pretty strong feeling that what we were doing was important and was helping others improve their lives in significant ways.

- A culture that insisted on treating everyone in a respectful manner. This meant in every direction – up, down, sideways, with those who were inside the organization and with those who weren't.

- A genuine desire to provide our people with the resources they needed so they could do their jobs well and to provide learning and growth opportunities for them.

- A strong effort to provide safe working conditions that were bright, clean, and pleasant places to be. Of course, a pleasant place to work is in large part a function of having people who are pleasant to be around – most of the time, at least.

- A genuine desire to improve – to become more effective at accomplishing our mission, achieving better results, and being better stewards of our resources.

Our organization was far from perfect. All of us make mistakes. Still, with occasional exceptions, our employees generally exemplified our desired culture reasonably well day in and day out. If that were not the case, I'm quite sure we would not have enjoyed the kind of successes we had.

# CHAPTER 6

## Building a Strong Financial Base

Four key decisions we made between 1986 and 1996 contributed significantly to Goodwill's strong financial position in 2015. The growing financial strength during those three decades, in turn, made it possible for us to take some risks and launch several initiatives that greatly multiplied our mission impact and transformed the entire organization.

Those four decisions involved our donated goods/retail operations, the oldest and by far the most visible part of Goodwill. It's important to note that the collection and sale of used goods was never intended to be primarily a way to make low priced merchandise available for poor people. Rather, the primary purpose of that part of the organization was to provide a largely self-sustaining means of creating job opportunities for people with limited vocational options. That remains the case with Goodwill in Indianapolis and many other local Goodwills and, thus, it is a means to an end – not an end in itself. In addition, to the extent that it is profitable, that part of Goodwill can often cover a large part of the organization's total overhead and support other mission-related services that are not self-sustaining.

In reality, though, when I arrived in Indianapolis in 1973, conventional wisdom was that people who would frequent thrift stores such as Goodwill's were those who had below average incomes. And, in fact, that was then the case with most of Goodwill's retail customers. But – in what could be viewed as a self-fulfilling prophecy - the primary reason was that the stores were in very poor neighborhoods. In those days most Goodwills tended to wait until other retailers moved out of a neighborhood and the rents dropped. Then Goodwill moved in. People who lived in those neighborhoods would shop in our stores, but few people who didn't live there would. Most of those stores were quite small and barely generated enough sales to cover their costs.

During the first few years I was CEO I closed several of those stores and opened larger ones in neighborhood shopping centers that had good parking. While I took some flack for doing that, the people who lived in the poorest neighborhoods still shopped with us. But by moving into areas where there were other retailers, we added a lot of new customers. And we began to understand why so many experts on retailing emphasized that the three most important keys to success were location, location, and location.

The decision to decentralize

Like nearly all other Goodwills, in those years we had a centralized system for sorting and distributing goods that had been donated by the public. At one time we had over 250 drop boxes on parking lots all over central Indiana. Our trucks went out from our main plant in Indianapolis, emptied the boxes, and brought the goods back to the main plant. There, we had a system of conveyor belts with 43 people stationed on them to sort particular types of clothing and household items. We also had extensive laundry, dry cleaning, and steam pressing facilities. It was an impressive site! And expensive to operate!

In 1976 the cost of dry cleaning fluid was increasing rapidly, and I decided to try an experiment that a few other Goodwills were also trying. Most of the clothing we received looked clean, and we knew that most of our customers would wash clothing they purchased from us before they wore it. So we stopped washing, dry cleaning, and pressing clothing. If an item looked clean and was in good condition we would put it in a store. Otherwise, it went into textile salvage. We tracked sales for several weeks and discovered that our clothing sales did not drop. But our expenses certainly did! We had learned that washing, dry cleaning, and pressing clothes added no value – only cost. That was the end of our laundry operations.

Over the next decade we also stopped repairing goods that had been donated to us. Small appliances had become throw-away items, and repairing other types of items (e.g., shoes, upholstered furniture) did not make economic sense. In nearly every case it cost us more to repair an item than we could sell it for. In addition, such repair operations no longer made sense from a job training perspective, as the labor market needed people with different skills.

In the 1970s gasoline prices soared, and the cost of operating our truck fleet went up accordingly. Labor and other costs also rose significantly, and by the mid-1980s we were barely covering the direct costs of collecting and selling donated goods. Two Goodwills actually ceased their donated goods operations, believing that there was no future in that business. Those would prove to be among the very worst strategic decisions ever made in those organizations, both of which eventually got back into the business. But they struggled to do so, as other organizations had moved into or expanded in their markets and become much stronger. Those Goodwills then had to compete even harder to build market share.

In retrospect, what both of those Goodwills failed to do was adapt to the changes that had been taking place in the world they were operating in. In sharp contrast, a few Goodwills had begun to experiment with decentralizing their donated goods operations. In essence, this involved encouraging donors to take their donations to a Goodwill store, where the goods would be sorted, priced, and sold. For several months, George Galyean and I evaluated the pros and cons of doing so in central Indiana. We knew that such a move would significantly reduce the number of jobs at our Indianapolis plant, and while we also knew that some of our people could make the transition to working at one of our retail stores, we were concerned about our ability to transfer some of those who had more significant disabilities to other positions in the organization. We did not proceed with decentralizing until we felt we could absorb elsewhere nearly everyone working on jobs that would be eliminated. Many of those employees were transferred to our Industrial Services Division.

The decision we made in 1986 to decentralize is one of the best decisions we made during my career. It greatly reduced operating expenses without reducing revenue, dramatically demonstrating that every time we touch, move, transport, or store an item we add no value – only cost. That decision set the stage for tremendous growth in our retail revenue and net income, greatly strengthening the organization's financial position, which – in turn – gave us the ability to expand our services.

<u>The decision to grow more aggressively</u>

For decades, the only competition for Goodwill's used goods business came from other not-for-profit organizations that used the same general concept to help them accomplish their missions.

But then some entrepreneurs discovered they could make a lot of money selling used goods. In fact, some of the most successful learned the business while working for another large not-for-profit. They went from "doing good" to doing very well.

We decided our best approach to the threat of competition from for-profit thrift store operators was simply to do a better job – to be more convenient for donors and shoppers, and to provide better service and better value. While we thought the approach of some of the for-profit thrift store operators was misleading to donors, we also realized that most of the donors didn't care. They were simply looking for a convenient way to dispose of the goods they no longer wanted. Most of the customers didn't care, either. They were just looking for the best bargains they could find and would patronize whoever provided what they were looking for. Most didn't care if it was run by a for-profit or a not-for-profit.

We also knew that some of the for-profit thrift store operators were well capitalized and had aggressive expansion plans. Unlike local Goodwills, they had no geographic limits on where they could operate and in some markets they were providing very tough competition for the local Goodwills.

In 1987 I decided to grow our donated goods/retail operations much more aggressively and try to become so dominant in the central Indiana market that those national for-profit thrift store operators would not target Indianapolis for expansion. They would go first for the low hanging fruit in other cities, and there was a lot of low hanging fruit out there. Where Goodwills were not expanding to build market share, they were leaving the door open for those for-profit competitors to do so and become an even greater threat to Goodwill.

My conclusion: Our best defense against the for-profit thrift store operators would be a strong offense. I was convinced that where there is money to be made, somebody is going to make it. In fields where Goodwill has competencies and it fits with our mission, I figured that "somebody" might as well be us. After that decision, we started adding donation centers and stores at a much faster rate.

The decision to buy land and build a store in an upscale community

In 1990 our donated goods/retail operations were expanding to more central Indiana communities, but we lacked a site in Carmel, an Indianapolis suburb that was (and remains) the most affluent community in the state. It was also growing rapidly. For months we had been trying to find a site where people could drop off their donations, but no one – not even the churches we contacted – would allow us to use any part of their parking lots. Finally, in frustration, we considered going just north of the Carmel city limits, buying a piece of land, and building a store that would include a drive-through donation center. We knew the donations would be there and that they would be of high quality, but we didn't know how successful a Goodwill retail store would be in that upscale area. The site we were considering was immediately across a highway from a newly developing center anchored by a Wal-Mart. We finally concluded that if our store did not prove to be successful we would probably have no trouble selling our building and getting our investment back.

Predictably, there was opposition, much of it from residents of the neighborhood just west of our chosen site. After three appearances before the Westfield Planning Commission, though, we received approval to build an 8,000 sq. ft. store.

The night before the store opened, we held an invitation-only open house. I noticed one gentleman I had not met before who walked all over the store, looking carefully at the merchandise. Finally, he came up to me and said, "I know some of these people (the neighbors) gave you some trouble, but don't worry about them. Give them a month and they'll all be in here shopping. I know these people, and they're all bargain hunters."

The store was an instant success and too small from the start. It took a decade before we were able to put together a deal that resulted in our building a much larger store immediately across the street. We then sold the original store for twice what we had invested in it.

This experience proved to us that if we located our stores where we were likely to obtain good quality merchandise from donors, we could sort it and sell it at the same location – often to the same people who were donating. There are bargain hunters at all income levels.

With the overwhelming success of the Westfield/Carmel store, we began buying land and building stores in other suburban areas. Leasing in those areas was still not an option for us in those years, as most developers did not yet consider Goodwill to be a desirable tenant. So we looked primarily where big box retailers were building and got as close to them as possible. In essence, we let those big retailers do our market research for us, and it worked every time. The return on our investments in those stores was phenomenal – much greater than we could have hoped for from other types of investments. More importantly, we were able to use the resulting financial strength to greatly increase Goodwill's mission-related impact.

Part of that impact was our ability to employ more people whose opportunities were quite limited, and there's no better example than Lorena Salas.

*Lorena first came to Goodwill in 1996 while attending the Indiana School for the Blind. In addition to being blind, she also has cerebral palsy. And she is one of the most delightful people you will ever meet.*

*Lorena organizes clothing on rolling racks that are used to transfer merchandise from the store's back room to the sales floor. It's not easy for her, as she has weakness in her hands and low dexterity. But she sets challenging goals for herself and is always trying to do more. She says, "I get really excited when I hit six racks because it helps keep the store organized and improves our customers' experience."*

*While Lorena takes her job seriously, her store manager says, "...she also loves to laugh and brings a lot of joy to the store." Lorena adds, "It's not about me. It's about the people we serve."*

Eventually, several developers began seeking us out, and as more good locations became available to us, we concluded that we could grow faster if we leased rather than tied up capital to build and own. Our preferred approach then became to identify properties, negotiate the deals, have a developer build a store to our specifications, and then lease it back from the developer.

This suburban strategy was a grand slam home run. While no one in Carmel would lease to us in 1990, by 2007 we had two stores open within the Carmel city limits – an indication of how much the situation had changed.

The decision to advertise

In 1996 our donated goods/retail operations were doing well – our sales were around $10 million/year, and we were doing no advertising. I began to wonder what would happen if we advertised. We started talking with knowledgeable people about this, and all of them told us we needed to be willing to spend at least 3% of our sales on advertising for at least three years or we would be wasting our money.

I gulped, but we then sought proposals from ad agencies and selected Young and Laramore, the one we thought might do the best work for us. I had second thoughts, though, after the agency came up with concepts for two television spots that I viewed as "off the wall." They were vastly different from anything I had envisioned, and I wasn't at all sure how a conservative Midwest audience might react to such an unorthodox approach. George Galyean, our Marketing VP Cindy Graham, and I had several discussions about this until one day they sat across from me in my office and said, "Jim, trust us on this."

I decided to give them the green light and take the risk, thinking that if we got an adverse reaction we could pull the spots, stop the campaign, and chalk it all up to experience.

I needn't have worried. The response was phenomenally positive. People loved the commercials, and we loved the results, as the "Goodwill Guy" advertising campaign helped generate a 25% increase in comparable store sales the first year. If only half of that was due to the advertising, we got our money back three times over that year. The campaign was still going strong when I retired 19 years later.

Occasionally during those years someone would ask me how we could afford to advertise like we did. My standard reply was that we couldn't afford not to.

Those commercials also prompted a major improvement in Goodwill's image in central Indiana and confirmed how little I had known about advertising.

This was definitely a grand slam home run.

## Cumulative Impact

The cumulative effect of locating stores with drive-through donation centers in areas that were convenient for middle- and upper-income households, along with our developing an immensely popular, long-running advertising campaign enabled us to take advantage of a cultural shift that was occurring during the same general time frame. During the first half of my career, most middle- and upper-income people rarely, if ever, bought used clothing. Most generally tended to avoid "second hand" stores, many of which were messy, poorly organized, dimly lit, and not always as clean as they should have been. As Goodwill and a few other thrift store operators gradually improved the locations, layout, signage, lighting, cleanliness, and general overall appearance of the stores, we attracted new customers who were looking for bargains. Over time, shopping in our stores actually became trendy among shoppers who could afford to shop anywhere they pleased. We benefited enormously from that broader base during the last half of my career.

## One other factor

Goodwill's financial position also benefited from the growth of an endowment that was started by my predecessor in 1971. Housed in a related 501 (c) 3 entity, Goodwill Foundation of Central and Southern Indiana, Inc., funds from the endowment were not available to subsidize day-to-day operations on an ongoing basis. The Foundation's growth was greatly enhanced by key decisions made by the Investment Committee in 1995 to invest for long term growth and spend no more than 5% of the average value of the corpus over a rolling three-year period for grants and expenses.

As it grew, the Goodwill Foundation became a wonderful source of seed money to help launch new ventures and services. In a sense, it served as Goodwill's own private equity fund. The Foundation has also helped with large capital projects, given many scholarships and internships, and provided matching funds for other grants received by Goodwill.

The additional financial strength we derived from the foundation gave us the freedom to take some risks we probably would not have taken otherwise. The overall results greatly enhanced and accelerated our organization's growth in size and impact.

# CHAPTER 7

## *You Win Some, You Lose Some*

In the 1990s, our organization was becoming bigger and stronger. We had learned a lot – or so we thought – from some of our less successful earlier ventures, and we believed we wouldn't make the same mistakes again. And, of course, we were always interested in creating more work opportunities for people whose options were limited by disability, criminal history, or other significant barrier.

And while we didn't necessarily make the same mistakes we had made earlier, we found ways to make new ones. At times, we didn't do enough due diligence. Sometimes, we didn't execute well. And at other times we made some assumptions that simply turned out to be wrong.

In this chapter I first describe four strikeouts. Then I'll provide examples of some initiatives that worked well – at least for a while.

### Losers

#### Nurse's uniforms

As I previously wrote, the AbilityOne program offers opportunities for qualifying organizations to manufacture products or provide services for the federal government as a means of increasing employment of people with significant disabilities. While, as I described in Chapter 3, Goodwill had considerable success fulfilling service contracts and manufacturing wood products under that program, our other attempts at manufacturing products for the federal government could best be described as humbling.

As the government's need for file boxes declined, we began searching for other products to make. In 1991 that search led to a contract to manufacture nurse's uniforms for the U.S. Department of Defense. The Miami Goodwill had a very large and successful industrial sewing operation under AbilityOne, and we concluded that if they could do it, so could we. In addition, I had some work experience in the apparel manufacturing industry while I was in college, so I thought I knew something about how to make such an effort successful. As it turned out, I didn't know nearly enough.

We hired an experienced sewing manager who relocated from a part of the country where, in sharp contrast with Indiana, there was a large industrial sewing industry. We ordered and installed equipment, hired and trained workers, and waited. Conflicting specifications within the documents provided by the government caused months of delays, and the government sharply reduced the size of the original order after we had bought equipment, but before we had started production. Finally, in 1993 we were able to begin producing. We made a very good product, but the reduced volume made it nearly impossible for us to break even, given that we had no other sewing business over which we could spread some of our fixed costs. In addition, the product specifications resulted in a much more complicated uniform than local hospitals were buying, and we were not even close to being price competitive with nurse's uniforms manufactured in Asia. Eventually, we were awarded a one-time contract to make trousers for the government, but the likelihood of additional orders of significant size was low. When we had filled all the orders, we shut down the operation and sold all the equipment.

Some of the problems associated with that contract were our fault; others were the fault of the government. We concluded, in part, we had selected the wrong product in the wrong industry at the wrong time. In the final analysis, we really had no one to blame but ourselves. This was by far the worst experience we ever had in any of our industrial operations.

Fortunately, other parts of Goodwill were doing quite well in those days, so the losses associated with the nurse's uniform debacle did not have a large effect on us. (Actually, I've conveniently forgotten how much money we lost on that venture – not to mention the amount of management time and attention it took.) And while our patient board seldom reminded me of any of our failures, occasionally over the next few years when I would present them with a proposal for a new venture, one of our directors would ask, "This isn't another nurse's uniform is it?" Usually, he would be smiling when he asked that.

I learned from all the initiatives we undertook. I generally learned more from the failures than from the successes. And, with one exception, I never regretted trying them. That exception was the nurse's uniform contract.

Major strikeout.

Expansion of space for Commercial Services

Since the 1940s, Goodwill in central Indiana has offered companies a variety of small assembly, packaging, and inspection services, as well as other labor intensive services, as a means of employing more people with significant disabilities. In more recent years, that part of the organization has also provided opportunities for people exiting the corrections system to join the workforce as they restarted their lives.

Always trying to grow that part of the organization, in the late 1990s we became the contract packager for a company that sold low margin safety products to large retailers. We leased 150,000 sq. ft. of space in an industrial park, moved equipment into it, hired employees, and began operating. We had leased over twice the amount of space we needed for that contract, but the economy was strong and we thought we could add other business that would fill up the plant. We were wrong. The economy turned south, and new business was very hard to attract. In addition,

- We did a poor job controlling our labor costs.

- We had accepted the customer's pricing at the start, and it took far too long to get price increases when it became apparent that many of the operations were grossly underpriced.

- There were far too many SKUs, with too many changes too frequently, and we didn't charge nearly enough to cover the cost of the changes.

- Because most of the products were coming from China and being sold in "big box" stores, there was little room for price increases.

- Because we had too much space, our fixed overhead was far too high for the volume we were generating.

After changing supervisors, plant managers, and eventually vice presidents, we told the customer they would have to find someone else to do the work. Shortly thereafter, they transferred most of it to a plant in Mexico. We terminated our lease and consolidated our remaining commercial services business in a building we owned.

Plastics recycling

In 1993 we purchased supposedly state-of-the-art polymer recovery equipment that would convert used plastic (e.g., milk jugs) into high quality reusable plastic pellets. We ran the operation for two years but could never achieve the quality level we needed to attract a price that would cover costs.

As we were to discover, the Ohio-based manufacturer had incorporated into the equipment some new technology they had developed but had not tested. When it failed to perform to specifications, they were unable to find ways to improve the equipment or process to achieve the necessary and promised quality. In retrospect, we had not done enough due diligence on the company, its owners, or the equipment before we decided to do business with them. Rather than continue to lose money, we sold the business to an Atlanta-based company that was consolidating small recycling operations such as ours.

Reverse logistics business

In 1998 the CEOs of the Milwaukee and New York City-based Goodwills and I began discussing whether the three organizations we were leading – three of the largest and strongest Goodwills in the country – could jointly develop mission-enhancing business opportunities that were beyond the capability of any one Goodwill. With the approval of our boards, we formed a limited liability company, Goodwill Services International, LLC, jointly owned by the three to seek out and develop such opportunities. Subsequent discussions centered around the field of reverse logistics, a type of operation with which the Milwaukee-based Goodwill had considerable successful experience.

A business relationship developed in 2000 with a well-established for-profit reverse logistics company that had a processing center in an Indianapolis suburb. As envisioned, the relationship would make available to Goodwill products that could be sold in Goodwill stores and provide work opportunities for Goodwill employees. A number of problems surfaced, though, including:

- The product mix was significantly different from what we had been told was likely.

- The volume was uneven and never sufficient to operate the processing line at capacity.

- The product that was obtained proved to be very marginal in Goodwill stores.

- The person at the partner company who had championed the project was fired for reasons unrelated to the project, and communications with that company were never consistently good thereafter.

Others within that company simply did not have the same level of interest in the project.

- The partner company had other problems, including serious difficulties upgrading its computer system and the need to close one of their offices. Those and other problems occupied their attention and made it difficult for them to give our venture the attention it needed.

A second company with which we had developed a reverse logistics agreement was a startup backed by a New York venture capital firm that had tremendous difficulty getting commitments from prospective customers. Consequently, we never had any business from that source.

Several months after we began operations, one of our partner Goodwills had issues that required more focus on its core operations, and we finally concluded it was best to terminate our reverse logistics contracts. While in theory we could have sought other opportunities, each of the three Goodwills had enough significant opportunities and challenges that we decided to cease our efforts to jointly develop one or more businesses. We hadn't invested much money in this effort, but all three of us CEOs had invested significant amounts of our time. One of our conclusions was that the amount of top management attention required to develop such businesses was not warranted by the size of the potential benefits to our organizations.

Some Winners

While I don't classify any of the following examples as home runs, all of them were solid singles or doubles. Overall, those are vital to having a good batting average. And ours was pretty good.

All these initiatives were managed by our Commercial Services Division.

## Recycling for a public utility

In 1990 we developed a joint venture with PSI, an Indiana public utility. We named the venture PSI Recycling. PSI provided management, Goodwill provided labor, and we recycled paper and cable. The operation reached a plateau after a few years, and our part in it ended in the mid-90s.

## Wooden reel manufacturing

In 1991 we secured a contract to manufacture large wooden reels. We invested $150,000 in a CNC (computer numerical control) router to do the work. It did not create many jobs, but it did generate a lot of revenue with good margins for three years.

## Blow molding and filling

In 1992 we entered into a relationship with a St. Louis company that sold windshield wash to large retailers. They did the product design and marketing from St. Louis, and we became their manufacturing arm. We bought some used blow molding and bottling equipment, installed two large tanks to hold the bulk solutions, hired a person with a lot of plastics blow molding experience, and began making plastic jugs and filling them with solution we blended at Goodwill. It was a very seasonal business, but during the busy season volume was quite high. After we had been operating successfully for several years, the company we were doing the business for had financial difficulties and could not pay their bills. At that point we ended the relationship and sold the equipment.

## Subsequent operations

In 2000, with a lot of learning from the experiences of the previous twenty years, I hired a new vice president, Jim Humphrey, to lead our Commercial Services Division. Jim had 16 years of supply chain management experience with a Fortune 500 consumer products company, and he took that part of our organization to new, much higher levels.

One of Jim's early projects was to lead us through preparations to become ISO certified, and we achieved ISO 9001-2000 registration in May 2002. That opened the door to development of sizeable, long-lasting relationships with several companies that have enabled Goodwill to provide a growing number of work opportunities for people whose options are very limited. While at one point I seriously questioned whether we should continue that part of the larger Goodwill organization, what I eventually saw is that with the right leadership, patience, and a reasonable level of ongoing investment, Commercial Services could add substantial mission impact and do so in a financially sustainable manner.

# CHAPTER 8

## New Dimensions for Retail

### Outlet Stores

In 2005 the Portland, Oregon Goodwill, which was the undisputed leader among all Goodwills in retail operations, was having considerable success with outlet stores they had developed. I sent Kent Kramer and one other member of our staff to Portland to study their operations. They came back convinced that we had huge undeveloped potential, and in November that year we opened an outlet store/distribution hub in a leased 100,000 sq. ft. building on the east side of Indianapolis. The retail portion occupied 11,000 sq. ft., with the balance devoted to warehousing and salvage operations.

The outlet store sold clothing and housewares by the pound. The more you bought, the lower the price/pound (with limits, of course). The goods were those that had not been deemed good enough to go into a "regular" Goodwill store or they had been in a store and didn't sell. By consolidating all such goods in one location and turning the inventory several times a day, we were able to greatly increase revenue from those items and greatly reduce the amount that might otherwise have gone into a landfill.

The store was an instant success. The customer base was quite different from that of our regular stores, so there was little, if any, cannibalization of sales. By 2008 we had opened two other similar operations that were equally successful in enabling us to extract considerably more value from goods that had been donated to Goodwill and divert substantially more material from landfills. This made us much better stewards of our resources – one of our Five Basic Principles. In addition, each of the three locations employed 85-90 people, many of whom had significant barriers. And the outlet operations enabled us to increase our net income, thus further strengthening our ability to support mission-enhancing services that did not cover their full costs.

The outlet stores/distribution centers were a grand slam home run.

## ecommerce

In 1999, Goodwill in Orange County CA launched shopgoodwill.com, an auction site that provided all Goodwills the opportunity to sell items over the internet. It proved to be a very successful way to expand our market and capture more value from some of the more unusual or highly-sought-after goods we had received from donors.

In central Indiana, we were among the early users of shopgoodwill. com, but we started quite slowly. Gradually, as we gained experience we started posting more items online. Our retail stores received credit for the goods they selected to be posted online, so our store managers had an incentive to sell items in the way that was likely to generate the highest yield.

In 2006, aware that we were not doing a very good job selling donated books in our stores, we launched eBooks. That operation also grew gradually as we gained experience.

Not long thereafter, we moved all our eCommerce operations into a dedicated 80,000 sq. ft. space which, by the time I retired, had hundreds of thousands of items and over 100 employees. Shopgoodwill.com remained the site for collectibles, jewelry, electronics, musical instruments, toys, dolls, games, and other items. Books and media eventually were sold on eBay's platform.

By selling online, our potential market became worldwide. While each Goodwill could still seek donated goods only from its assigned geographic territory, we could sell online to people anywhere. While I do not envision online retailing ever totally replacing physical Goodwill stores, it seems reasonable to assume that ecommerce will continue to grow (it soared during the COVID-19 pandemic), generating an increasing percentage of the total revenue Goodwill earns from the sale of donated merchandise.

Grand slam!

# CHAPTER 9

## *The Business or the Mission –*

## *Which is More Important?*

While, as I wrote in an earlier chapter, I learned more from the writings of Peter Drucker than any other author, the book I found most helpful was Built to Last – Successful Habits of Visionary Companies, by Jim Collins and Jerry Porras (HarperBusiness, 1994). The authors studied companies that had managed to thrive – not merely survive – over long periods of time, and they looked for commonalities. Two of those really struck home with me:

- The visionary companies had constancy of purpose and a few core values, but everything else – their business models, products and services, organizational structures, policies, processes, even their cultures – changed over time.

- The visionary companies did not "brutalize themselves with the tyranny of the OR – the view that says you can be A or B, but not both." Instead, they "embraced the genius of the AND – the paradoxical view that says you can be both A and B, even if they are seemingly contradictory notions."

For me, this confirmed what I had long believed about the importance in our organization of excelling from both business and mission perspectives. Early in my career, there was an ongoing debate among some of my colleagues around the country about which was more important – the business or the mission. I never quite understood why those who asked the question thought we had to make a choice between the two. Finally, when I read Built to Last, I knew we didn't have to.

It was certainly true that if we didn't pay enough attention to the business side to maintain an adequate financial position, eventually we wouldn't be in business. It was equally true, though, that if we didn't have significant mission impact, it's doubtful there would be any justification for us to continue enjoying a privileged not-for-profit tax status.

I took the position that if we were going to excel over a long period of time, we had to be able to perform at a very high level in all our various operations and services – those that were mission-enhancing businesses and those that were mission-focused services that had a smaller or even no business component. To some, this might have seemed to be a paradox. But I believed we had to be able to reject either/or thinking and embrace paradoxes such as:

- Having a purpose beyond profit AND pragmatically pursuing a level of profit that enabled the organization to be financially sustainable.

- Having a clear vision and sense of direction AND being opportunistic.

Rejecting either/or thinking in our organization, we worked to:

- Excel from both business and mission perspectives.

- Retain an entrepreneurial spirit and build a strong, dynamic, serving institution.

- Manage constant change and maintain a reasonable amount of continuity.

- Maintain a strong institutional memory <u>and</u> benefit from a lot of fresh ideas, insights, and perspectives.

- Employ and develop leaders with strong business skills <u>and</u> a strong commitment to the mission and the people we assisted.

- Operate with some of the advantages of a large organization <u>and</u> retain some of the advantages of smaller ones.

- Do well in both the short term <u>and</u> long term.

- Optimize innovation <u>and</u> maintain a reasonable degree of stability and security.

No one ever suggested that any of this was easy. And while not everything we tried succeeded, I'm quite sure we did much better over time than would likely have been the case if we hadn't taken this approach. I also took the position that if we were going to err, I would rather it be from having tried to do too much than not enough.

# FOOD FOR THOUGHT

## *Perception vs. Reality*

*T*oward the end of my career, we had become – for a not-for-profit – quite a large organization. Our size had many positive aspects. It enabled us to attract a higher level of managerial and professional talent than was possible before, and that in turn enabled us to become substantially more productive and effective. Our heightened capabilities made it possible for us to greatly enhance the scope and quality of our mission-related services and develop new approaches that significantly increased our long-term impact in the lives of people and the communities in which we operated.

But there was also a downside.

The bigger and more visible we became, the bigger target we were. In addition to having a lot of employees, students, and people served in various other parts of our organization, we had two million donation transactions and four million customer transactions a year. Bottom line: We had a lot of opportunities to make people like us or mad at us. And nearly all of them had access to social media.

We had also become a complex organization that had been changing rapidly. Regardless of how much we had done to tell our story, most people had no idea of much of what we were doing. Perception always lags reality.

Goodwill is certainly not the only organization that experiences a significant gap between public perception and reality. Almost any of us could say something similar about the organizations we are connected with. Even if we once thought we understood someone else's business, organizations that *survive over long periods of time aren't standing still. They're changing in ways that are often not visible to the general public. The faster the rate of change within the organization, the greater the gap is likely to be between what the organization is and how the public perceives it.*

Compounding the challenge for us was the reality that, while our organization was composed of a lot of wonderful people doing some terrific work, we were made up of more than 3,000 human beings, and not one of us was perfect. All institutions have flaws, and despite all the good work we were doing and all the improvements we had made, there was nothing we were doing that couldn't be improved even more.

During most of my career, we periodically had independent surveys conducted to determine how we were perceived by the general public. Those surveys consistently showed well over 90% favorable public opinion. I described the remainder as falling into one of four categories:

1. ***The uninformed or misinformed.*** *Some people didn't like us because they didn't know enough about us. This category included those who had erroneous assumptions that logically led to incorrect conclusions about our operations and services (and sometimes about our competence and integrity).*

2. ***The aggrieved.*** *These are people who had had a bad experience with Goodwill. I subdivided this group into two categories:*

   a. ***Those who were unhappy with a decision we made or an action we took,*** *even though we had acted responsibly and were fully justified in our actions (e.g., some personnel decisions). There wasn't a lot we could do about those in this category other than ensure that the decisions we made and the way we operated were consistent with our values and based on sound criteria and sound processes.*

b. *The justifiably aggrieved. These are people with whom we had made a mistake or simply not treated well. Obviously, we could reduce the number of people in this category by constantly improving our performance. And when we did become aware of a mistake we had made, we tried to correct it as quickly and fully as possible, do our best to make amends, and remember to say, "I'm sorry."*

3. **The philosophically opposed.** Goodwill has not historically encountered a lot of opposition on philosophical or ideological grounds. However, in our efforts to provide opportunities to certain populations or address a particular social problem, we did occasionally encounter people who simply did not agree with our position or direction. While we might never win the support of some of those individuals, we at least tried to do our best to explain the rationale behind our positions and directions.

4. **The jealous.** The larger and more successful we became, the more we were likely to encounter individuals who were simply jealous or resentful of our success. There will always be some people in this category, and we can't control that. But we did try to guard against adding to their number by treating everyone with respect, by not acting or appearing arrogant, and by not bragging.

*It's almost axiomatic that it's much harder to build than to destroy:*

- *Nearly any human-made object*

- *An organization*

- *A reputation*

- *Trust*

*Those who are inclined to damage or destroy the reputation of or trust in an individual or an organization have more tools available to them today than ever before. And at times, the court of public opinion does not wait for evidence before rendering judgment.*

*We always hoped that those who talked or wrote about us – whether through social or mass media – would treat us fairly. Our positives far outweighed our shortcomings, and we hoped for perspective, a sense of context, and balance. If someone publicly called attention to a flaw or a mistake someone in our organization had made, we hoped they would give proportionate attention to the good things we did. We also knew, though, that in this day and age such hopes are usually unrealistic. As negative emotions tend to be stronger than positive emotions, negative stories seem to attract a lot more attention – viewers, listeners, readers - than positive stories.*

*So how should those of us in leadership positions respond? Part of our approach was to constantly seek more effective ways to increase awareness of our mission-related services and impact. But there's more. With greater size comes greater responsibilities, and we sought to hold ourselves to an increasingly higher standard. There was never any room for complacency.*

*And regardless of how others – individuals or media outlets - might treat us, we tried to continue to treat others as we would want to be treated, keep our focus on the work to be done, acknowledge and correct our mistakes when we made them, and continue to uphold the values and basic principles by which we operated. And we sought to become ever better stewards of all our resources as we worked to help improve lives and strengthen communities. Because – even if not everyone always recognized it - that is who we were.*

# CHAPTER 10

## Characteristics of A Highly Effective Board

We never could have achieved what we did without the kind of board I served under.

The Indianapolis-based Goodwill was formed in 1930 and incorporated in 1934. From 1934 till 2015 it had only three CEOs. The first, Howard Lytle, was there 34 years and retired. The second, Alan McNeil, was there 4-1/2 years and died way too young. I was there 41 years and retired. (Obviously, it's a dead-end job!) However, the success of the organization throughout that long history has been due more to the quality of the board of directors and the relationship between the board and CEO than any other factor.

Lytle deserves a lot of the credit. Early on, he attracted a significant number of high caliber people to serve – individuals with a lot of knowledge, skills, experiences, more than an average amount of wisdom, and a strong appreciation for Goodwill's values and mission. Many were leaders in their fields and in the community. As a group, they provided steady guidance and leadership for the young organization and helped establish its position in the community. Many of them served for long periods of time, and they also attracted other high caliber people. Goodwill continues to benefit from the foundation the early directors established.

While we were always able to attract and keep first-rate people to serve on our board, the size of the board and the way it functioned changed as the organization grew and evolved. The composition of the board also changed over time in response to changes in the external environment, including changes in the prevailing culture of our society and societal expectations of not-for-profit organizations.

I readily acknowledge that one size does not fit all. But because we had such a good experience at Goodwill Industries of Central Indiana (GICI), perhaps a description of our board and how it functioned – especially during the latter part of my career - will be useful to others. I'm referring here to the board of GICI. Two related entities, Goodwill Foundation of Central Indiana, Inc. and Goodwill Education Initiatives, Inc. had separate boards that differed in size and composition from the board of GICI. Mechanisms were always in place, though, that enabled us to keep all three entities aligned.

In 1992 our board adopted a document that specified the responsibilities of the board and expectations of individual members of the board. The preface to the board's responsibilities read:

"The board is the organization's governing body. It should be concerned more with long term than short term matters, matters of policy rather than operational concerns, and matters of paramount rather than ordinary importance."

Of course, a board must ensure that structures and mechanisms are in place to maximize the probability that the organization will comply with applicable laws and regulations. While the board has ultimate responsibility, from a practical perspective the CEO and his/her staff must see that on a day-to-day basis the organization is operating in a manner that will not only accomplish the organization's mission, but that will also keep it out of trouble with regulatory bodies and law enforcement agencies. The board must do all it can to ensure that the CEO it selects has the values and skills necessary for the organization to function in a way that enhances its long-term viability. I agree with those who believe that the hiring of the CEO is the board's most important function.

Specific responsibilities of the board included:

1. Hire and monitor the performance of the President/CEO.

2. Monitor the key indicators of the organization's performance.

3. Periodically review the mission of the organization and the degree to which the mission was being fulfilled.

4. Establish policy.

5. Approve strategic plans.

6. Approve annual plans and budgets.

7. Approve new programs and business ventures that created or had the potential to create significant obligations for the organization.

8. Ensure financial solvency and access to adequate amounts of capital.

9. Enhance the public standing of the organization.

10. Interpret the organization to the community, and vice versa.

11. Assess its own performance.

Expectations of individual members of the board included:

"Each member of the board should make every effort to attend board meetings and to participate on committees and task groups. Regular attendance is necessary if one is to remain knowledgeable about Goodwill's activities, capabilities, plans, and major concerns. Board members also are expected to make known their areas of particular interest and/or expertise and to volunteer to be utilized by the organization in those areas of interest and expertise."

In participating, board members were encouraged to:

1. Ask questions (especially the hard questions) and make suggestions.

2. Constructively critique and challenge others as appropriate.

3. Be willing to support the majority in a spirit of cooperation.

4. Make judgments based on what is best for the organization as a whole.

5. Understand the role of the board as a policy making body and avoid becoming involved in operational matters.

6. Avoid actions and involvements that might damage the organization's reputation or be harmful in other ways. Understand and adhere to the organization's Conflict of Interest Policy.

7. Introduce the organization to others who might be able to assist the organization.

8. Check personal agendas at the door.

The division of labor between board and staff is not static. It changes as the organization grows and adds more competencies to its staff. Generally, the boards of startups and other small not-for-profits must be more hands-on than is necessary or desirable in larger, more established organizations. In our organization there was a gradual change in the types of decisions made at the board and staff levels as the organization grew and evolved. Matters that would have been considered large and worthy of the board's attention twenty years earlier would later be considered a waste of the board's time and were handled by staff. Board agendas in the last decade of my career were considerably different than they were even a few years earlier.

When I arrived in Indianapolis as a very young executive, Goodwill had a wonderful board of directors and no forced rotation system. Terms were three years, but there were no term limits. The average age of those on the board was probably in the late 50s or early-60s, and my greatest fear was that they would all grow old and die at the same time and we'd have to start over. Of course, that didn't happen, and we never did establish term limits. That approach worked because we managed the nominating process and took great care to understand what skills were needed and what contribution each person on the board was making. Our Governance Committee (which had responsibility for nominating candidates for officers and directors) had the courage not to invite those who were not making a significant contribution to stand for re-election to another term. They made some tough calls from time to time, but they always put the best interests of the organization first – even if it meant that occasionally someone got his/her feelings hurt. I have seen few not-for-profit boards with as much courage, and I am convinced that, year-in and year-out, the Governance Committee (aka Nominating Committee in many organizations) is the most important committee a not-for-profit board has. If you get the right people, a lot of other things will fall into place.

In addition, we occasionally elected people who had served well for long periods of time, and who continued to be interested and active, to the position of Honorary Director. We continued to invite each of those persons to all board meetings, although they no longer had a vote. But along with the perspective, insights, and institutional memory those persons provided, we were able to attract others who brought new ideas and perspectives. The combination worked well for us.

People on most not-for-profit boards are not getting paid to serve, so it's particularly important that they enjoy the experience and get some intangible rewards for their service. Part of enjoying the experience is a function of how well those on the board work with each other. Chemistry on a board matters. Diverse perspectives are vital, and members should not all be on the same social level. If too many are too close to each other, one member might be too hesitant to take a position against another member. And a board that succumbs to group think is no more likely to excel than a board that is unable to lead effectively because it is constantly at war with itself.

Before each Governance Committee meeting called to identify or consider potential board members, I prepared a memo that included:

- A description of the organization's current operations.

- Growth opportunities and significant challenges – current or anticipated.

- My assessment of skills, perspectives, access, etc. that we should consider adding to the board.

- Other matters for the committee to consider.

I participated in Governance Committee meetings and sometimes suggested persons for consideration. But the committee members controlled the process and outcomes.

While the new members of our board had generally had experience on other boards, it was important that they received an in-depth orientation to our organization and the way we functioned.

Because our organization had over 3,000 employees and operated three very different types of businesses, it was important that we had on our board some people who were or had been CEOs or other high-level executives in companies of comparable size or larger. Those persons were usually in a better position than most to understand the dynamics and challenges of running a large, multi-division company. Also, it was particularly important that the board's leadership be "big picture" thinkers and not nit-pickers. They needed to be able to see the organization in a larger context. Where did it fit in the larger community? Where did it fit within the fields in which it operated?

Because we had close working relationships with organizations in all three sectors – for-profit, not-for-profit, and public – we also strived to have people on our board who understood the various sectors. The nature of our organization also made it important that we have access to high levels of state and local government and be able to work effectively with government regardless of which political party was in power. The makeup of our board generally reflected most or all of those needs. So it was a fairly diverse group of people. But they also respected and worked well with each other. Because we had people of high integrity who, when they were involved with Goodwill, put the organization (and not their own personal agendas or interests) first, we were able to accomplish this even among people who in other aspects of their lives were often on opposite sides of issues.

In only one instance in my career did I see a board member's ego adversely affect his/her ability to be effective with our organization. Others on the board recognized and dealt with the matter, and that person resigned from the board.

Boards composed largely of people elected or appointed by the people or groups they represent may be an appropriate (perhaps even the best) form for the public sector and for membership-based associations that derive most of their revenue from the dues paid by their members. However, I do not believe that is an optimal board composition for organizations that operate in a competitive marketplace or that really want to overcome the lack of market forces to excel. Such boards are often too large, but regardless of their size they are often composed of people who may be competing for resources or who have other conflicting interests or agendas. This can result in slow decision-making processes and often a lot of compromise. The slow decision-making processes make anything more than incremental change very difficult to accomplish absent a severe crisis, with the result that they frequently lag economic and technological realities. It is extraordinarily difficult for such organizations to excel over time.

People stayed on our board in large part because they enjoyed the experience. They also found it interesting and rewarding. There were several reasons for this.

First, we tried very hard not to waste their time. Of course, every meeting takes staff time as well as board time, and we didn't want to waste our time either. Consequently, over the years as our internal competencies increased, we reduced the number of standing committees to three (Governance, Finance and Audit, and Compensation) and increased the use of ad hoc committees or task groups. We also made sure we didn't call committee meetings unless we really needed them. One of my most embarrassing moments in a board meeting came early in my career when a kind, wise man on our board made a report for a committee that had met just prior to the board meeting. His report consisted of one sentence I will never forget: "Nothing occurred at the meeting that requires action, and very little occurred that doesn't." I got the message loud and clear.

We wanted board members involved where they could truly add value. As with paid employees, volunteer board members will be happiest and most productive if:

- Their values and the values of the organization are compatible

- They strongly agree with the organization's mission

- They can use their skills, abilities, perspectives, and other resources to make a contribution

- They can learn and grow

- They enjoy the people they work with

We generally tried to structure our agendas around important issues. If a meeting consists of nothing but reports on what has happened since the last meeting, it is probably a waste of everyone's time. There are many ways of conveying information that are much more efficient than bringing a lot of people together in one place.

I believe the Pareto Principle (i.e., the 80/20 rule) is useful in many situations, including board meetings. For example, you might try to spend, on average, no more than 20% of the time at a board meeting reviewing the past so you can devote at least 80% to looking ahead. This will, of course, vary from meeting to meeting.

It's terribly important to keep the board informed, but to do so in a way that respects their time. Providing too much information can be as bad as not providing enough. We constantly sought to strike a balance likely to keep people informed, interested, and involved, but not to the point where we became a burden to them. It was also important to remember that boards don't like surprises – unless they're happy ones – especially if they first learn about them in the local news media.

The key to a successful meeting is preparation. For a CEO, this requires knowing what you want to accomplish at a meeting, sending relevant information out in advance, discussing key issues with key people in advance, and trying to anticipate everything that might come up and determining how you would handle it. Such preparation increases the likelihood that you will be able to have good discussions on significant agenda items, make good decisions, and end the meetings on time. On the relatively few occasions when our board did not agree with an action I had recommended, it was usually because I hadn't done my homework. They didn't rubber stamp.

I took the lead in drafting board meeting agendas, discussed them with the board chairperson, modified them based on the chairperson's input, and then distributed them prior to the meetings.

My direct reports usually attended the board meetings, and during the latter part of my career one of our board chairs told me they wanted to hear more from my staff than from me. They knew me and my capabilities, and they wanted to get better insights into the abilities of my direct reports.

I was happy to comply, and that change turned out to be good for me, our executive team, and the board.

Not only is the chemistry within the board important, so is the chemistry between the board and the CEO. Fortunately, over the years I seldom had problems working with members of our board. On one occasion, one of our directors – a very successful entrepreneur – thought we weren't opening enough stores. He told me I should push our staff more. I told him it was my job to know when and how far to push our staff and when to back off. At the time, we were growing rapidly, and some of our key people were stretched very thin. You can stretch people only so far for so long before something gives. It's my job to sense that and to manage accordingly. He listened, understood, and never brought the subject up again. A couple of years later he strongly encouraged me to pursue a new venture that would further expand our revenue base. As it happened, we had thought of the same idea, but had not acted on it. His encouragement gave us enough impetus to develop the concept, which turned out to be very successful. His style and mine were radically different. His style was better suited to the smaller companies he ran very successfully, but mine was better suited (in my opinion) to running a large, diversified not-for-profit. Despite our differences, his contributions during his years on the board were valuable.

Of course, the relationship between the board chair and the CEO is particularly important.

The first chair of the Indianapolis Goodwill's board of directors held the job for 25 years. The chairperson in office when I became CEO held the job for seven years, the next one for three. We then established a pattern of having the chair serve for two years. That worked well for us. In most situations I believe two or three years is about right. One year is generally too short (but can be an effective way for the CEO to enhance his/her job security), and more than three can result in the chair's beginning to tire of the responsibility. There are exceptions, though, particularly if the organization is searching for a new CEO or is in the midst of a crisis and needs continuity of leadership until the crisis passes or a new CEO is reasonably well established. A longer term is also often advantageous in startups. Of course, the smaller the board, the more necessary it might be for the chairperson to hold the position longer (unless, of course, everyone who is brought onto the board has the ability and willingness to lead it at some point).

There may be some situations in which a person can chair the board for long periods of time without some unintended negative consequences. Too often, though, if one person "owns" the job for a long period of time, others do not develop the level of interest and involvement they might otherwise have. It's important to be concerned about depth of leadership and succession planning at the board as well as the staff level, and good Governance Committees will keep that in mind.

We were fortunate in having a wealth of talented people to consider for board leadership posts. We generally designated a Chair-elect one year before a person assumed that office. Other than that, we had no pattern of "working through the chairs", as do some organizations. I'm not opposed to that pattern; we just chose not to use it. Another organization I was associated with has a pattern of one-year chairpersons, and in that case "working through the chairs" made a lot of sense. When I chaired that organization, we made sure all of those coming up for the next three years were involved in all strategic decisions so we could plan more than one year out.

Because the chemistry between the board chair and the CEO is so important, our Governance Committees always took that element into consideration when nominating board officers. They always asked my opinion (for which I will forever be grateful), and I was never reluctant to offer it.

Of course, because the chemistry between a board chair and the CEO depends so much on mutual trust and respect, it is vital that a CEO never do anything that would in any way undermine that trust and respect. There is also always the danger that the relationship between the board chair and the CEO might become too cozy. A relationship in which hard questions don't get asked or pursued is just as bad as one in which there is constant criticism and nit-picking. The optimal blend is a friendly, but professional relationship in which the board and the CEO are both focused on doing what is best for the organization and its mission.

Some of our board chairs had their own preferred way of working with a CEO, and some wanted more involvement than others. Part of my job was to understand how they wanted to work and what they wanted of me. My objective was to do whatever I could to make their years as chair an enjoyable, rewarding experience for them. Of course, the best way for me to do that was to ensure that the organization performed well, that we stayed financially strong, and that we avoided actions that might damage our reputation.

Both the board and the staff have a responsibility not only to do good work today, but also to ensure that the organization continues to be relevant in periods of rapid change. It is vital that an organization's board periodically assess its own viability in the context of current and anticipated future challenges and opportunities and ensure that its structure, composition, and the way it operates provide the organization with the best chance to excel.

# CHAPTER 11

## A Perspective on Performance-based Compensation

## in a Mission-Driven Organization

*Not everything that counts can be counted, and not everything that can be*
*counted counts.*

William Bruce Cameron (often attributed to Albert Einstein)

A s the not-for-profit sector has grown over the past few decades, expectations of not-for-profit organizations – especially the larger ones – have also increased substantially.

In the early days of my career, many people would support organizations just because the people working in them had good intentions. Then we began to see an increased interest in activity metrics – e.g., number of people "served", hours of counseling provided, etc. - metrics I consider to be indicators of "busyness." Even citing "job placements," a key metric used by many Goodwills, leaves a lot to be desired. More information is needed, such as (1) the increase in earned income resulting from the placement, and (2) some minimum length of time the job lasted before being counted as a "placement."

Then along came a heightened emphasis on accountability – mainly in the financial sense. But you can be accountable for every penny you receive and spend and still be totally ineffective. More recently, though, we have begun to see much greater interest in indicators of impact. For example, how many people are benefiting, and to what extent are their lives changing for the better? In some fields, measures of economic impact might also be desirable. In other words, can we quantify the economic return the community receives for its investments in the form of charitable contributions and tax dollars received by the organization?

In addition to heightened expectations of demonstrable impact is an increased expectation that not-for-profits will be good stewards of their resources, which requires good management. To meet all these greater expectations, many not-for-profit organizations must be able to attract and keep people with the same level of knowledge and skills that are in demand in other sectors. This can be very difficult if there is also a widespread belief that people in the not-for-profit sector should work for substantially less money than they could receive for doing similar work in a for-profit company of similar size and complexity. This problem is compounded by the low value many funders place on any functions other than direct services to people – especially those functions that constitute the dreaded "overhead."

Another relevant factor to consider is that competition between not-for-profits and for-profits for business as well as talent has increased in recent decades, and that movement has gone in both directions. Some not-for-profits now generate a greater share of their revenue from the sale of products and services that compete with similar products or services offered by for-profits. And some for-profits have gone after the more lucrative niches of services that were formerly provided primarily by not-for-profits.

As a result of all these factors, compensation levels have increased in many not-for-profit organizations – especially the larger ones – and in many cases have become more comparable with those of for-profits of similar size and complexity. In what may be the biggest understatement in this book, this trend is not universally embraced. (For a powerful position on that and related topics, see Dan Palotta's book, <u>Charity Case: How the Nonprofit Community Can Stand Up for Itself and Really Change the</u>

<u>World</u> (Jossey-Bass, 2012), or just watch his TED Talk "The Way We Think About Charity is Dead Wrong.")

At Goodwill in central Indiana, we tried very hard to have compensation systems that enabled us to attract and retain the level of talent that would enable us to excel in every aspect of our work, but that would still be viewed as "reasonable" by knowledgeable people. However, I nearly always took the position that if compensation was the most important factor for a person, they should go elsewhere. There would always be another company that would pay more. Besides, you never build equity in a not-for-profit organization.

I also wanted, as much as possible, to tie pay to performance. But it couldn't be based solely on financial performance. That might work in a for-profit company, but it would not be appropriate or desirable in our not-for-profit organization. In addition, I wanted to have a variable component of compensation that could fluctuate and not have people expect that they would automatically get an increase every year.

It has long seemed to me that if a substantial part of a person's pay (or their continued employment) depends on hitting a number, many (most?) people are going to find a way to hit the number. We've seen far too many examples in all the sectors of the damage that can be done when such systems aren't properly designed and implemented. So for quite a long time, when I thought about trying to design and insert a variable pay component into our executive compensation system, I took the safe (or, depending on your point of view, cowardly) route and did nothing.

Eventually, I started trying to design a variable pay component for our executives, and I worked on it off and on for several years before I thought I had something that might work and – very importantly – we had enough confidence in our data systems to try it. My biggest concern, of course, was that if we didn't properly design it the system might encourage actions that would not be in the best interests of the organization or the people we served. Finally, we came up with an approach that worked reasonably well. It wasn't perfect, and parts of it were modified and refined a bit every year. While some of our executives thought it was too complex (and they might have been right), it was generally well-balanced and did what it was intended to do.

Some of its features were:

- The plan was designed to be "pay-at-risk" or the "variable pay" portion of total compensation for executives. Base salaries were set so that, with the addition of the maximum allowable bonus amount (never more than 20% of base salary), total compensation would remain within the target range established by the Compensation Committee and approved by the Board of Directors.

- While it was always necessary to balance short- and long-term interests, it was crucial that the plan not encourage short term actions that were likely to damage long term development or in any way adversely affect the organization's reputation. Consequently, the CEO, in conjunction with the Compensation Committee, reserved the right to modify or eliminate any or all payments if there was any indication that actions were taken that were not in Goodwill's best interests, that could have potentially damaged the organization's reputation, or that violated Goodwill's values and basic principles. The CEO and Compensation Committee interpreted all provisions and made the final decisions regarding awarding of any payments.

- Payments were made on a prorated basis if consolidated operating income fell between the target (100%) and threshold amounts. Factors considered in determining threshold amounts included:

  - cash was available to meet all debt service requirements and budgeted capital expenditures,

  - appropriate accruals were established and maintained,

- a sufficient level of working capital was maintained.

- The amount of incentive payments was determined based on the year-end financial statements and paid as soon as practical thereafter.

- There were two payout components:

  - A strictly objective component that was determined by actual performance related to goals for key metrics. This accounted for approximately two-thirds of the total payout.

  - A more subjective component that was recommended by the CEO, subject to the approval of the Compensation Committee. It considered accomplishments that supported strategic objectives – especially those that had potential for significant long-term benefits for the organization and people served by the organization – but that might not have contributed to short term results during the current year. This component also considered progress toward other objectives previously discussed by the CEO with the executive and other factors related to the executive's overall effectiveness. This component was designed to account for approximately one-third of the total payout.

- Goals, metrics, and targets were set in advance for each executive position and were weighted. Every position included financial and mission metrics, and most also included metrics related to other important considerations (e.g., safety, customer satisfaction).

- Metrics for executives of support functions as well as the CEO included some that were for the organization as a whole. The idea behind this was to provide an incentive for staff in those departments to do all they could to help the revenue-generating, mission-enhancing parts of the organization achieve their goals. This was one way we tried to ensure that our internal bureaucracy served as an enabler and not a hindrance to the accomplishment of important overall goals.

The executives who participated in this system – my direct reports – were so committed to the organization that the impact of this system on their performance was most likely marginal. However, it did serve as a constant reminder of what we considered most important and, therefore, valued most highly. An additional benefit was that the discussions on their performance within the Compensation Committee gave its members much greater insight into the strengths and weaknesses of each of my direct reports. Those additional insights became increasingly important in succession planning, particularly as I approached retirement.

Systems such as this must be tailored to fit each organization. One size does not fit all. We must also remember that with even the best designed system, changes are sometimes needed during the year because of circumstances that could not be foreseen and were beyond anyone's control. There should be an overriding desire to be as fair as possible to the individuals who are affected, while also guarding against adverse effects to the organization.

If this had been easy, we would have done it long before we did.

# FOOD FOR THOUGHT
## *Optimizing*

*W*hile I frequently described Goodwill's overall objective in general terms as "Maximizing mission-related impact while maintaining a financial position that enhances long term viability," the overall challenge was really one of optimizing – finding the right balance.

Many of our management challenges involve finding optimal solutions. For example, how much of our revenue should we spend on General and Administrative expenses, i.e., overhead? Some people believe not-for-profits should minimize G&A, and many funders will pay little or nothing for overhead. In the long run, that is a recipe for ensuring mediocrity at best, as it results in inadequate value-added support of the high mission impact parts of the organization. Spend too much, though, and there could be legitimate questions about whether the organization is being a good steward of its resources. In this, as is in so many situations, one size does not fit all. Two very important factors in arriving at an optimal percentage are the size and complexity of the organization.

Another example: One of Goodwill's historic roles has been to provide work for people whose options are limited by disability, criminal history, low education level, or other significant barrier. This has been a very important part of our mission and one way we can add unique value in a community. Obviously, then, we want to provide as many jobs as possible for individuals who don't have many options. However, because retail is the financial backbone of the entire organization and operates in a highly competitive marketplace, we must have enough people with skills that enable us to be competitive *and efficient. If we do not have enough people with barriers who have the necessary skills, we must hire others who can fill the gap. In the latter part of my career, filling approximately 2/3 of the jobs in donated goods/retail operations with people who have employment barriers generally seemed to result in an optimal mix.*

*There's another optimizing challenge embedded in that example, though, and that is the mix of full-time vs. part-time employees. We always had quite a few employees who for any of a variety of reasons were not able or simply did not wish to work full time. However, if we had too few full-time employees, overall productivity could drop, and that would affect financial performance.*

*External factors can also have a powerful influence on optimization challenges. Changes in laws or regulations that significantly increase operating expenses can make it necessary to reprioritize and determine a new optimal mix of operations and services and/or full-time vs. part-time employees that would enable Goodwill to continue meeting its overall objective of maximizing mission-related impact while maintaining a financial position that's good for long term viability.*

*Nothing is static. Conditions are constantly changing, and we must constantly adapt or suffer the consequences. Optimization issues are always before us, and we must always strive to find the best balance point – at least until something else changes.*

# PART III

*Evolving*

# CHAPTER 12

## Genesis of a Transformational Evolution

In 1990, Goodwill Industries of Central Indiana, Inc. was generally viewed by Goodwill leaders around the country as one of the more successful Goodwills in North America. With $9.4 million in revenue and 671 employees, we were the 10th largest of 165 independent, locally governed and managed organizations that were members of Goodwill Industries International (GII). Our 29-county territory represented the 35th largest market in population among Goodwills. We had what for a local Goodwill was a somewhat traditional mix of operations and services with 14 retail stores, some commercial services operations, and some job training, vocational rehabilitation, and job placement services. Most of the people we worked with and employed were adults with disabilities.

As I wrote in the introduction, twenty-five years later, with revenue exceeding $130 million and 3,300 employees, we were the 4th largest of 164 local Goodwills. The substantial growth, though, was not nearly as significant as how the organization had evolved to increase its long-term impact.

The rate of evolution began accelerating when we opened a charter high school in 2004. However, the process that led to that catalytic event began about 15 years earlier, most of it under the leadership of one of our vice-presidents, Byron Jensen. Byron had an extensive background in human services, and through his experience leading the Indianapolis Community Service Council he was particularly well connected with leaders in the not-for-profit and public sectors in central Indiana. Byron had initially joined Goodwill to help me with a capital campaign and strategic planning. He brought intellectual energy and was fun to work with. He and George Galyean became good friends as well as co-workers, and the three of us worked closely together throughout the 1990s and into the early 2000s revamping and growing the business and mission sides of the organization.

Byron led numerous initiatives that broadened our scope, and every major move we made built on what we had learned from prior experiences – our own as well as the experiences of others. Perhaps most importantly, all those major initiatives were in an effort to increase the organization's long-term impact.

While since World War II Goodwill's focus had been primarily on people with disabilities, in the late 1980s our target populations began to broaden. The driving force behind the change was very low unemployment in central Indiana and consequent difficulty employers were having filling their vacancies. Some of those employers were calling us, practically begging for people. There was also a growing interest in doing more to help move people on public assistance into jobs, and in 1989 the head of the state agency that administered welfare asked us if we could help do that. We conducted a pilot program and found that we could move welfare recipients into jobs, but generally only the lowest paying jobs because most of them lacked high school diplomas. Still, we continued providing welfare-to-work services for the next 17 years and at one time were the largest welfare-to-work service provider in the state.

After federal welfare reform legislation passed the U.S. Congress in 1996, there was a large increase in federal funding to move welfare recipients into jobs. Sensing an opportunity, some entrepreneurs based elsewhere formed companies to do just that in various cities across the country. Indianapolis Mayor Steve Goldsmith, a proponent of privatizing public services, helped two of those for-profit welfare-to-work companies obtain contracts in Indiana. I was quite unhappy that our mayor had brought in those companies that would be competing with us, and I told him so. But we quickly realized that whether we liked it or not, we had new competition and had better quickly decide how we were going to handle it. Our conclusion was to do all we could to provide better service and better value for the state, which was paying the bill. The competition lasted several years until the welfare rolls had been reduced to a point where the market could no longer provide viable opportunities for all of us. The for-profits left town, and we continued providing those services as needed for several more years.

During the 1990s we also began to develop partnerships with other organizations in various Indianapolis neighborhoods. One of the most successful was with the John Boner Center, a social service organization on the near eastside of the city. We jointly developed the Career Corner, in which Goodwill staff provided employment-related services, and the Boner Center's staff provided various wraparound services needed by those who went to the Career Corner for help preparing for and finding jobs.

That was the first focused alliance where we leveraged the complementary strengths of two organizations to create a new capacity that would expand and improve services in a neighborhood. The success of that effort, which continued for 11 years, stimulated the development of other relationships with entities in all three sectors – public, for-profit, and not-for-profit - to leverage resources and cause some good things to happen that otherwise probably would not have happened.

Another example was with what at the time was known as Clarian Health Partners (later to become Indiana University Health), which operated three hospitals in Indianapolis. Together, we created JobLink to provide soft-skills and job-specific training to candidates for entry level jobs at Clarian. For people assisted by Goodwill, JobLink meant opportunities for employment with potential for long-term career growth. For Clarian, it meant a more effective way to recruit and hire qualified entry level workers.

As our people gained experience working with each other, we developed additional joint programs, including one where we provided training and English lessons for Clarian employees with limited English language capabilities.

Other alliances we developed in the late 1990s and early 2000s that were successful for at least three years included:

- Career Academy at the Blue Triangle. Goodwill provided vocational/employment-related services to previously homeless residents of a transitional residence operated by Partners in Housing.

- The Airline Industry Recareerment Project, which Goodwill developed in response to the large number of layoffs in the airline industry following the 9/11 terrorist attacks. Partners included Indiana Department of Workforce Development and Indiana State AFL/CIO Institute for Training. Funding came from state and federal sources. During the project over 400 persons who had been laid off attended basic computer classes and over 600 participated in occupational skills training.

Our most successful working relationships with other organizations were those in which:

- We and our partner had a common goal with clear, measurable objectives around which the relationship was built.

- We had compatible values.

- We had complementary resources and capabilities.

- We trusted each other. (There can be no success without this.)

We also had to bear in mind that a successful relationship could be undone because of a change in one key person. In reality, we don't have relationships with other organizations; we have relationships with individuals in those organizations. When key players change, we must develop relationships with the new players.

Moreover, the mutual trust and respect among the partners must go deeper than just board to board or CEO to CEO. Effective working relationships and trust at multiple levels are essential. We never had any success when the CEOs of the organizations were in favor, but key people at lower levels were not.

While our focus in the early 1990s had remained primarily on employment-related services, some of our experiences were causing us to begin thinking much more about the impact of low education levels on employment. In particular, as I described in Chapter 3, for several years beginning in the mid-1990s, we operated the one-stop employment service centers in Indianapolis, which saw 40-50,000 unemployed people each year. When we started examining demographics, we were shocked to discover that 50% of them did not have high school diplomas. It was also readily apparent that a substantial percentage of those who used the services of those centers were frequently cycling in and out of the system – some of them several times a year.

Also in the mid-1990s, the public was becoming aware of the true extent of the dropout rate in some of the city's high schools, and we began wondering if, as an organization, we had anything to offer young people who weren't headed in a positive direction. We figured if we could help them stay in school and get a high school diploma, those young people would be less likely to need Goodwill's services once they became adults. Therefore, the organization's long-term impact in the community would be greater.

We became involved in several small-scale initiatives, all of them with the Indianapolis Public School system (IPS), the largest of eleven school corporations in the county. One of our greatest learning experiences during that time came from a program we designed that we called TechWest. TechWest was a three-year pilot program we developed with Northwest

High School (NWHS) to see if we could improve the success rates of students the school's staff deemed highly likely to drop out. Approximately 40 students a year came to us as second semester sophomores and spent two semesters in the program at Goodwill. NWHS provided two teachers and a social worker on a part-time basis, and IPS provided the transportation. Goodwill provided instruction leading to a computer-related certification, and a Goodwill employee taught life skills classes. We also arranged for internships for some of the students and provided summer employment programs for those who wanted to participate. We raised over $900,000 from private sources to pay for the program for three years.

TechWest was successful in improving the academic performance and attendance of the vast majority of the students, and most of the students who completed the program earned industry recognized certificates in computer-related disciplines. However, at the conclusion of their year with us, the students had to return to NWHS – the environment in which they had previously struggled – for their final three semesters of high school. While we provided a staff person at the school to help students with the transition, most of them regressed.

IPS agreed with us that it would be preferable for the students to remain in TechWest until they graduated. But they still wanted us to continue the program as is. We told the IPS Superintendent we could not try to raise funds from private sources to continue what we all now knew was a flawed program. When the IPS Superintendent told us they could not provide any public funds for the program, we told him we would have to discontinue it at the end of the third year. We also told him we knew we had something to offer young people who were not headed in a positive direction and that we would likely explore possibilities under Indiana's new charter school law. He then stated directly to Byron and me, "If you apply for a charter, you become our enemy."

We were stunned but proceeded to learn more about the charter law. When we ended TechWest a few months later, IPS publicly lambasted

Goodwill. The Indianapolis Star's education reporter contacted us, and we told her the full story. She chose not to believe us, though, and the next day the Star ran a front-page story above the fold with the headline "Goodwill shuts down popular IPS program" which contained false statements from IPS. I was livid. The CEO of the Indianapolis Chamber of Commerce called me and said, "Jim, they don't know how to collaborate." The head of the mayor's charter school office reminded me that "no good deed goes unpunished." Our board of directors remained fully supportive of us.

The day after the story ran, the reporter called us to say that staff at Northwest High School had contacted her and said that what we had told her was accurate. However, the newspaper never ran a correction or retraction. (A few months later, IPS hired that reporter to be its media spokesperson.)

Taking the advice of our Marketing VP, I resisted my instincts to fight back, recognizing that if we publicly bashed IPS, the only beneficiary would be the newspaper. The kids we were all concerned about would certainly not benefit. And our primary supporters knew the full story.

We had learned a lot, and we knew we had something to offer. But it was clear that at least for the foreseeable future, any education efforts we made would not involve IPS. (Note: A few years later, with a different school board and a new superintendent at IPS, the situation changed dramatically for the better.)

In 2001, Indiana's legislature and governor had made charter schools possible. The new law gave the Mayor of Indianapolis chartering authority, and Mayor Bart Peterson had embraced that law to help improve public education in the city. He asked David Harris to set up a charter school office, and in 2003, during the last school year we operated TechWest, Harris had approached me and asked if we would consider starting a charter high school. He and the Mayor wanted to get some strong local organizations more involved in education improvement efforts, and they wanted to bring to the city some education models that had been developed and implemented elsewhere but did not exist in Indiana.

After several months of discussion with many knowledgeable people, our board voted unanimously to apply for a charter. Our application was approved by the City-County Council 28-1, and in August 2004 GICI opened the Indianapolis Metropolitan High School with 116 freshmen. From the beginning, the school served a high poverty, high special needs population of students.

Starting that school was – by far - the hardest initiative I have ever taken on. But the launch of the school was the catalyst for an incredible organizational learning experience and a rapid increase in the rate of Goodwill's evolution. From the outset, we began to encounter societal problems we had known existed but had never had to confront directly. We soon saw that if we didn't help some of the students deal with some of the problems they were facing outside of class, they weren't going to be in class. The home situations of some of the students were abysmal. A few had been abandoned by both parents. Ten to fifteen percent of the female students were pregnant or already had babies. By the second year I was no longer surprised at anything I heard about the challenges some of our students were facing. As a result, though, we began wrapping services around some of the students and sometimes members of their families.

We also began to appreciate the vital importance of every student's having a positive, long-term relationship with at least one responsible adult. Such relationships had not existed in many of the students' lives.

Toward the end of the somewhat chaotic first year, it was obvious to me, as well as to others at Goodwill, the school needed new leadership. At the suggestion of Dan Riley, our Chief Financial Officer, I talked with Scott Bess, who was serving as Goodwill's IT Director, about becoming Chief Operating Officer of Goodwill Education Initiatives, the related 501(c)3 entity we had established for Indy Met and any additional schools we might develop. Scott had previously taught and coached high school students and sat on the board of his local suburban school district. He had a passion for education and jumped at the opportunity. That turned out to be one of the best internal leadership moves in my career.

While a lot of learning was taking place (by the staff as well as the kids), we wanted to better understand some of the issues we were dealing with. Four years after opening the school, Eric Lange, a very bright recent college graduate, joined Goodwill, and I asked him to do some research into the links between poverty, low education levels, crime rates, births to young unwed mothers, and a host of health issues. Eric soon came back with an enormous amount of data showing the extent to which those problems are frequently inter-related and often reinforce and compound each other. Yet, as a society, we generally treat them in isolation one from another.

The public sector tends to do this through large, bureaucratic silos that often don't communicate effectively with each other. On the other hand, the not-for-profit sector is incredibly fragmented, consisting of hundreds of thousands of organizations, most of them small. Many of them do good work, but each is typically focused on only a piece of a larger, more complex set of issues, and we have not been very good at connecting the pieces. Overall, we tend to be program-rich and systems-poor.

We then began doing more serious thinking about what we might do in response to what we were learning. Questions we frequently addressed included:

- Where do we fit in the communities where we operate?

- Where do we fit in the fields in which we're engaged?

- How does what we're doing relate to what others around us are doing?

- What's happening outside the organization that could affect what we do or how we do it - that might create an opportunity or pose a threat?

Another vital question we frequently considered is "How can we have the greatest impact in the lives of people and communities?" A related question soon became even more important:

How can we add unique value?

If others could do what we were doing as well as or better than we were doing it, is that how we should be deploying our resources? Shouldn't we be able to find a way to use our assets and capabilities to add unique value in a community?

We also reinforced our overall objective in general terms as "Maximizing mission-related impact while maintaining a financial position that's good for the long-term viability of the organization."

And we articulated a set of general directions and preferences to use as a guide in decision making:

- We strive to offer services that result in long term impact.

- We prefer to develop long term relationships with those we assist.

- We seek to incorporate holistic, whole family approaches with those we assist.

- We emphasize the enhancement of education levels and the attainment of credentials that improve an individual's employability and earning potential.

- We strive to prevent problems and develop potential.

Overall, we aspired to help reduce multigenerational poverty and the array of social problems associated with it, and everything the organization did was intended to play a part in helping individuals and families increase their economic self-sufficiency.

This process of questioning and learning led to the development of The Excel Center - the greatest innovation to date in the history of Goodwill in central Indiana. And that is the subject of the next chapter.

# FOOD FOR THOUGHT

## *On Cross Sector Competition*

*W*hile in the 1980s we had responded to rising competition from for-profit thrift store operators, when for-profit welfare-to-work companies entered our market and began competing with us in the mid-1990s, we did some serious thinking about cross sector competition.

It was clear that the increased movement of for-profits into fields that formerly were occupied solely by not-for-profits as well as movement of not-for-profits into commercial ventures that competed directly with for-profits was usually for the same reason: to make money. The for-profits were often seeking the lucrative niches of fields that traditionally had been occupied primarily by not-for-profits, and the not-for-profits were seeking new ways to raise money to support their missions.

Even when it was not about making money, it could still be about money. A good example is the competition some public school corporations have from charter schools, which are publicly funded, but privately operated. Frequently, when those associated with public school corporations express their dislike for charter schools, what they are really concerned about is competition for students and the money that follows them. My view is that we need both high performing traditional (e.g., district operated) public schools and high performing charter schools. It's even possible for them to work closely and effectively together, as has been the case with some of the Innovation Network Schools that have developed in recent years under the Indianapolis Public School system.

*Some of our conclusions about cross sector competition were:*

- *Neither morality nor competence is determined by or reflected by an organization's tax status. Some organizations in each sector are very good; others are not. There are highly competent, highly ethical people in each sector. Unfortunately, one can also find some incompetent and unethical people in each sector.*

- *Where the sectors seem to be converging, the competition is often for talent as well as for customers or students.*

- *Competition can make us better.*

- *Many organizations underestimate the difficulty of developing a new competency.*

- *If you don't have the capital and talent to be competitive in a venture without harming your ability to accomplish your primary mission, stay out of the business. Or – form an alliance or merge with an organization with complementary resources and capabilities.*

- *In the final analysis, I believe that for many direct human services, people and communities are often better served by well-run not-for-profits than by government or for-profit companies. Still, either of those might be better than a poorly run not-for-profit.*

*Our approach was to adhere to applicable laws and regulations, price our products and services fairly, do the best job we could, and let the marketplace decide if that was good enough.*

# CHAPTER 13

## *The Excel Center*

None of the students who entered Indianapolis Metropolitan High School at age 18 or 19 with few credits succeeded. They needed a different kind of school. Moreover, through Eric's research we had become aware that 14% of the adult population in the city and state lacked a high school diploma. Education options for them had been few, and most of those led to a GED. However, data showed that few who started a GED preparation program successfully completed it, and other research showed that those for whom a GED was their highest level of education attainment made no more money and were employed at no higher a rate than high school dropouts.

Scott Bess and his staff went to work designing a school that would fit the life circumstances of adults who lacked high school diplomas. The result was The Excel Center®. A lot of changes were made during the school's first year, additional tweaks have been made in subsequent years, and features of the model now include:

- Accelerated eight-week terms, with rolling enrollment throughout the year.

- Individualized learning plans and flexible scheduling.

- Life coaches to help students stay on track academically and to help find solutions to non-academic problems that might affect a student's ability to remain in school.

- Opportunities to earn free college credits and industry-recognized certifications.

- Free on-site childcare for the young children of students while they are in class.

- Hands-on internships and job training.

- Job placement with private sector employers.

The first Excel Center opened in September 2010 with 300 students. With no advertising, six months later there were 2,000 people on the waiting list. We added two more sites in 2011, two more in 2012, four more in 2013, and two more in 2015. During the 2014-15 school year, enrollment in nine schools in five different communities totaled nearly 3,000, and over two-thirds of our graduates had earned an industry-recognized post-secondary credential by the time they received their Excel Center diplomas. All the Excel Centers were charter schools funded through a line item in the state's budget rather than as part of basic K-12 funding.

Growth has continued since my retirement. Partly through licensing arrangements, ten years after the first school opened there were 31 Excel Center locations across five states and Washington, D.C. More than 6,300 students had graduated; 61% of those had earned an industry-recognized certification, and 38% had earned college credits. Funding mechanisms have varied from state to state.

While there is a wide age range among the students, 61% have school-aged children, and there is an important two-generation component to the Excel Center. Because of the dearth of good, accessible, affordable childcare alternatives, the free on-site childcare available at each Excel Center location eliminates a huge impediment for many students, quite a few of whom dropped out of school the first time around when they became pregnant. After we opened the first school, we saw how happy the young children were to come to school with mom or dad. But when graduation came around, we really began to understand how important the Excel Center is to the next generation.

At each graduation while I was Goodwill's CEO, I had the privilege of sitting on the stage and seeing the proud faces of the children of graduates as they watched their mom or dad walk across the stage in a cap and gown and receive their diploma. And I am convinced that those kids will never forget that moment. I say that having watched my dad receive a college diploma two weeks after my fifth birthday. That memory is still vivid in my mind, and I've often wondered if being there at that moment is why I always knew I would go to college – even though I don't remember anyone ever telling me that was something I should do.

At one Excel Center graduation ceremony, one of the graduates was a 46-year-old mother, and her two teen-age sons, both of whom had dropped out of school, were in the audience. The mother was one of the graduation speakers, and at the end of her three-minute speech, she took off her glasses, looked at her sons, called them by name, and said, "All right, your momma can do this. There's no excuse why you can't." Both of them subsequently enrolled in The Excel Center and graduated.

The oldest graduate to date is a 70-year-old grandmother. After the ceremony I asked her why she had done it. She told me she had constantly talked to her grandchildren about the importance of education and began to feel like a hypocrite. She said, "I had to do this." It took her two years, but she earned all the credits and passed the end-of-course assessments required by the State of Indiana, and she got her high school diploma. What a great example for her grandchildren!

Terri is another terrific example:

*Growing up, Terri's household did not place much value on schooling. "My family is pretty old-school, and we lived in the country," she said. "High school just seemed like a waste of time when I could be working or actively helping out somehow. My parents withdrew me from school when I* was 14 and said they'd homeschool me. Eventually, I withdrew from school completely at the age of 16."

Terri soon became a mother of two. She worked as a housekeeper, but after several years of cleaning houses, she sustained a severe shoulder injury from continuous, hard-scrubbing motions. Pregnant with her third child and now facing a second surgery to repair the damage to her shoulder, she knew she needed a change.

A conversation with her 10-year-old daughter made her realize that change had to start with returning to school.

"One day, I was trying to get my oldest daughter up for school. She was arguing with me, saying that school didn't really matter because she wasn't going to college or anything anyway...and it just broke my heart," said Terri. "Poverty perpetuates poverty, and I was witnessing my daughter giving up before she even really gave herself a chance. I'd seen ads for the Excel Center on Facebook and knew that is where I needed to start the change and set an example for my kids and myself."

After enrolling, she knew she had found the right fit. "The staff, even the other students, are all so supportive," she said. "Looking back, I wish someone had pulled me aside as a teenager and asked me what was going on. Luckily, I had the support I needed at the Excel Center. They build a whole community and safety net around you. Once I realized they weren't going to let me fail, I began to thrive."

Within a year of enrolling, Terri went from having zero high school credits to earning 40 and graduating with a 4.2 GPA. She was the top student in her class and even gave the commencement speech at her graduation ceremony.

Two months later, Terri landed a job at a large company headquartered in Indianapolis. And she will soon graduate with an associate's degree in accounting from Purdue University Global. After that, her company will move her to the finance department and support her future educational goals through tuition reimbursement for her bachelor's degree.

*"I honestly never thought I would be where I am today," said Terri. "The Excel Center not only prepared me from an educational standpoint...I jumped into college courses with no problem...but they gave me the confidence to pursue my dreams. They encouraged me to apply for a job that I worried I wasn't qualified for, and now I am doing better than I could have ever imagined."*

Data show that the children of high school graduates are far more likely to graduate than are the children of parents who do not have a high school diploma. Even without the data, though, I believe that the impact of the Excel Center on the children – and in some cases the grandchildren - of the graduates will be even greater than on the graduates themselves.

While I believe the ultimate indicator of the effectiveness of a school is how well the graduates do in the next phase of their lives, we need to also recognize the positive impact a school such as the Excel Center has on the next generation.

The Excel Center has been a grand slam home run – one of the most significant in Goodwill's entire history.

# CHAPTER 14

## *Nurse-Family Partnership and Goodwill Guides*

As a result of the research that we began in 2008, we were interested in learning more about any program or service that had solid evidence of significant long-term impact. One such program that came to our attention was Nurse-Family Partnership (NFP), a home visitation program for first-time mothers in low-income households who voluntarily enroll no later than the 28th week of pregnancy. A bachelor's or master's prepared registered nurse then goes into the home on a weekly or biweekly basis from that time until the child is two years old. In addition to addressing health-related issues, the nurse also spends much time helping the mother and, where possible, the father learn good parenting skills and how to create an environment in the home that's conducive to the proper health and development of the child.

NFP was created in Colorado in the 1970s, and its approach fits well with what is known about brain development during the first few years of life. The program has been the subject of several randomized controlled trials that have shown substantial long-term impact in a number of different areas, including:

- 60% reduction in infant mortality

- 56% reduction in emergency department visits for accidents and poisonings

- 48% reduction in child abuse and neglect

- 50% reduction in language delays of child at age 21 months

- 67% fewer behavioral and cognitive problems when the child is age 6

- 59% fewer arrests of children at age 15

- 53% reduction in alcohol, tobacco, and marijuana use ages 12-15

- 72% fewer convictions of mothers

- 82% increase in workforce participation of moms


Studies have shown that every dollar invested in Nurse-Family Partnership saves $5.70 in future costs for the highest-risk families served. (See additional information toward the end of this chapter for more on NFP's long term impact.)

While NFP operated in over 30 states, Indiana was not one of them. We worked for three years to find a way to bring it to the state. I had no interest in Goodwill's operating the program; I just thought the state needed it.

Finally, in 2011 funding was secured from the federal Maternal, Infant, and Early Childhood Home Visiting Program, with the money going to the Indiana State Department of Health. ISDH, however, asked Goodwill to operate it. With our very strong internal infrastructure, I knew we could do it, so we agreed. Four years later we had over 600 moms and expectant moms enrolled, nearly 1,000 babies had been born to participating moms, and 34 bachelor's and master's degreed registered nurses were on our staff. (Note: Since my retirement in 2015, Goodwill's Nurse-Family Partnership has expanded into several other parts of Indiana.)

Shortly after we began operating NFP, we began to see the incredible synergies that were possible with other parts of Goodwill. A high percentage of the young moms (median age 21) lacked a high school diploma, so we could link them with education opportunities through the Excel Center. We could also offer employment services through Goodwill's TalentSource unit, and relationships we had developed with major health systems in the area, as well as with childcare providers, housing agencies, and others enabled us to provide or arrange wrap-around services for participating families. Staff called Goodwill Guides provided the continuity in the relationship and helped link families with services they needed.

Frances and Danielle are two examples of Goodwill's Nurse-Family Partnership services:

### Frances

*When Frances became pregnant with her first child, she had a lot of uncertainties, questions, and anxieties. She heard about Nurse-Family Partnership, inquired, and enrolled.*

*"Navigating pregnancy and motherhood for the first time can be scary and intimidating. Having a registered nurse assigned to me to answer my questions and relieve some of my worries was very helpful," said Frances. "My NFP nurse also told me about another program at Goodwill that could provide additional support to help me start my career."*

*That program connects young adults ages 16-24 with a career navigator who offers support and guidance related to education, training, or transition into the workforce. For Frances, it meant she could participate in Certified Clinical Medical Assisting training at no cost to her. That led to her earning an industry-recognized certificate in a field where demand is high.*

*After Frances earned her certificate, Goodwill's TalentSource team connected her with an externship at a local hospital.*

*"Having an opportunity to gain hands-on experience working as a medical assistant gave me the confidence I needed to begin applying for positions in the field," said Frances. "My certification, the skills and confidence I*

*gained from the training and externship experience have all contributed to my gaining a position as a medical assistant at an Indianapolis hospital."*

## Danielle

*Danielle was a teenager when she became pregnant. With no car or stable living environment, she moved into a home for single mothers and their children. She also enrolled in Nurse-Family Partnership.*

*"My nurse provided me with the resources and information about what to expect while I was pregnant and after my son was born," she said. "She helped me feel more prepared for his arrival."*

*With no high school diploma, Danielle also enrolled in the Excel Center. "I knew school would be even more difficult once my son was born, and I wanted to get it out of the way," she said. "The Excel Center is flexible and works with students based on their needs, so I was able to accelerate my coursework."*

*During all of this, Danielle also juggled a job. "My nurse encouraged me to focus on the positive and keep moving forward," she said. "I knew I could count on her for support."*

*After graduating from the Excel Center, Danielle moved into her own apartment and was able to transfer jobs to a location closer to her new home. Her primary concern now is providing a safe, nurturing environment for her son, while also striving toward her goal of enrolling in a nursing program at the local community college.*

In November 2019, Pediatrics, a peer-reviewed journal of the American Academy of Pediatrics, published an 18-year follow-up of participants in a randomized clinical trial of Nurse-Family Partnership. According to NFP's national office, youth who had participated in NFP had, at age 18, significant improvement in cognitive functioning compared with youth in the control group.

Outcomes included "improved math achievement scores, receptive language abilities, working memory, and ability to read others' emotions. In addition, the nurse-visited youth were three times as likely to graduate from high school with honors compared to the control group. Also, at age 18, the proportion of nurse-visited youth receiving supplemental security income (SSI) for disability was 64.2% lower than that of the control group.

Moreover, nurse-visited female children born to all mothers participating in Nurse-Family Partnership, as a trend, had fewer convictions at age 18 than female children in the control group."

An additional 18-year study of high-risk mothers who had participated in nurse home visits during pregnancy until their child's second birthday showed that "when their first child was 18 years old, they had saved the government $17,310 (2009 dollars) in public benefits compared to women in the control group. These savings came from reduced costs for Medicaid, the Supplemental Nutrition Assistance Program (SNAP), and welfare cash assistance. Considering the $12,578 cost per family of program participation, this represents a net savings of $4,732 (2009 dollars) in government costs."

### More on Goodwill Guides

In addition to working with NFP families, Goodwill Guides were also made available to Goodwill employees with barriers and often to graduates of Goodwill-operated schools. The guides help find solutions to problems such as inadequate housing, transportation, childcare, or other factors that are adversely affecting an employee or graduate. Guides can also help develop career plans. Guides help arrange needed services, ensure the services are coordinated, and provide continuity in the relationship. Indy Met, which has continued to evolve into a "best fit" school for students with barriers such as homelessness, involvement in foster care, pregnancy, or parenting, uses guides known as family empowerment coaches who help make wraparound services available for families of students. The school also provides free on-site childcare and transportation assistance for students.

Laura provides us with one example of the kind of help Goodwill Guides can provide:

*In 2018 Laura enrolled in the Excel Center and began working part-time in a Goodwill store. She was also assigned to a Goodwill Guide.*

*Her Guide helped her find a solution to a vexing problem – she had no reliable transportation and did not know how to drive. She said, "I didn't want to learn how to drive at first, but my Guide was there to give me the support and encouragement I needed to get my license."*

*Not long thereafter, Laura was promoted to a full-time position and was able to buy a car. "Now I don't have to depend on anyone to drive me around; I can go wherever I want."*

*With continued support and guidance from her Guide, Laura graduated from the Excel Center with a high school diploma and was promoted to a department lead position at Goodwill.*

*Her Guide said, "Laura's always had a plan. She just needs someone to believe in her. Working together, we can make sure she has the support and guidance to achieve her goals and follow her dreams."*

# CHAPTER 15

## Connecting the Pieces

## And Winning the World Series

The Excel Center and Nurse-Family Partnership have been grand slam home runs. Each has major long-term impact, and each is financially sustainable at current levels of funding. But link those with Goodwill's employment services and wraparound services facilitated by Goodwill Guides – connect all those pieces in a coherent way and with continuity of relationships between those being assisted and those providing assistance – that's when it all comes together and – continuing with the baseball analogy – you win the world series.

Goodwill's business and mission operations really came together during the last few years of my career. With closer working relationships across our various operations and with other organizations that offered complementary services, we began to function much like an array of networks. Those included:

- Business development and employment services (including donated goods/retail, commercial services, federal service contracts)

- Education services (including Excel Centers operated by Goodwill Education Initiatives, Inc., the national network of Excel Centers, and Indianapolis Metropolitan High School)

- Health and family and other mission-related services (including NFP, disability services)

Those networks were supported and often linked by shared services, most of which had grown largely to support GICI's retail operations. I would like to say that all of this was the result of a grand plan, brilliantly conceived and flawlessly executed, but that simply isn't how it happened. It was an organic process that was constantly evolving.

At the time I retired, we identified three ways Goodwill was adding unique value in central Indiana:

- By providing employment opportunities for a lot of people whose options were limited by disability, felony record, lack of a high school diploma, or other significant barrier. This is a historic role for Goodwill, and two-thirds of GICI's 3,300+ employees had one or more of those barriers. Nearly half were the primary source of income in their households.

- By helping older youth and adults earn high school diplomas and post-secondary credentials and become established in the work-force. The Excel Center offered a unique and very effective way to do this.

- By leveraging GICI's resources with those of others to help develop and implement effective approaches to improve the health and well-being of individuals and families and help reduce some major social problems.

The third in this list was exemplified by Nurse-Family Partnership and the array of other entities that helped provide the whole-family, two-generation wraparound services frequently needed by NFP families.

Looking at all this a bit differently, we were working to help:

- Raise education attainment levels of undereducated young people and adults.

- Increase workforce participation and economic self-sufficiency of people whose options were limited by disability, criminal history, low education level, or another significant barrier.

- Improve pregnancy outcomes, child health and development in low-income households.

- Improve K-12 education options in Indiana.

- Make more effective use of existing resources in the public and not-for-profit sectors.

Populations we worked with included:

- People with disabilities

- People with criminal records

- People with no high school diploma

- First-time expectant mothers and new moms and their young children in low-income households

- Others with significant barriers that limited their employability

Yet, as I looked at Goodwill's early history, it seemed the organization might have been coming full circle. For example, in the late 1930s, the small Goodwill organization in Indianapolis worked with other organizations in the community to make available:

- A kindergarten

- A prenatal clinic

- A well-baby clinic

- A dental clinic for school children

- In conjunction with a local hospital and medical society, a home-based health care program

- Classes for female heads of households. Topics included childcare, food preparation and purchasing, and how to run a household while a spouse is in prison.

- Music classes for children

- A library with books mothers could borrow to read to their children

Of course, they also offered employment in Goodwill stores.

Goodwill's approach then was whole person, often whole family. Across the country, Goodwills began moving away from that approach in the early 1940s with U.S. involvement in World War II and the need to focus on increasing productive use of all resources to meet the challenges of the times. Following the war, many returning veterans used the G.I. Bill to get a college education. The rapid increase in the workforce's education level and peacetime applications of technological advances that were developed during the war contributed to increased specialization in nearly every field—including Goodwill's.

Overall, large segments of our society became better and better at dealing with smaller and smaller pieces, but in many cases we did not do a good job connecting those pieces.

During that period, Goodwill made a conscious decision to focus its efforts primarily on people with disabilities—particularly their need for jobs, as they were often the last hired and first fired. The Indianapolis Goodwill concentrated on professionalizing its operations and services and became a leader in the growing field of vocational rehabilitation. Other needs of employees and their families, while not totally ignored, often took a back seat.

Many other human services organizations also became more specialized. Newly formed organizations generally chose to concentrate on only one type of service or serve only one target population. Over the next several decades, the number of new and often highly professional not-for-profit organizations in the U.S. skyrocketed, but the fragmented sector that resulted became increasingly expensive and far less effective at reducing complex social problems than might have been the case with a more connected process.

The increasingly fragmented approach to human services after World War II was influenced by another important factor. The president, chair, and CEO of General Motors had created an organizational structure that was emulated by many large units of government, not-for-profit organizations, and corporations. Hierarchical, and with multiple silos, that structure worked well for several decades.

Eventually, though, with the constantly shifting external environment, adaptability became more essential than efficiency. General Stanley McChrystal describes this superbly in his book *Team of Teams: New Rules of Engagement for a Complex World* (Portfolio, 2015).

We now have the benefit of much more knowledge than in earlier decades, and some organizations are very good at some of the pieces. However, we're still not connecting the pieces well enough to substantially reduce some of the big social problems.

The way Goodwill in central Indiana has been evolving might serve as an example of how pieces could be connected more effectively. Characteristics of Goodwill that have been crucial to the way the organization has evolved have included a strong infrastructure, the job base and financial stability provided by a well-run donated goods/retail business, a lot of talented people, and a lot of relationships with people in many other fine organizations across all the sectors in central Indiana. In other cities, an organization with a different combination of core capabilities might be able to be an effective hub or backbone organization that would:

- Create a network – a coalition with strong local leadership that might include a combination of public, private, and not-for-profit resources

- Keep the various parts aligned toward the common goal(s)

- Provide support as needed to the various players

- Track and analyze data and make adjustments as needed

Organizations that would be key players in such a network need to see themselves in a larger context and might have to view themselves, their roles in their communities, and their relationships with other organizations in their communities differently from what might have been the case in the past.

However, to the extent they can combine and leverage complementary resources and strengths, the collective impact over the next 15-20 years could be enormous.

In all of this, though, the primary concern must be that people and communities are well served.

(For more on this topic, see my book *Toward Greater Impact - A Path to Reducing Social Problems, Improving Lives, and Strengthening Communities.*)

# FOOD FOR THOUGHT

## On Mission Creep

*I*n the not-for-profit sector, the idea that organizations should avoid "mission creep" or "mission drift" is conventional wisdom.

I believe, though, that this "wisdom" is one of the reasons for the extreme fragmentation of the not-for-profit sector that renders the sector less effective than it otherwise might be in substantially reducing major, complex social problems.

It's not that I think organizations should try to do more than they can do well. Not-for-profits that try to offer too many different services than are warranted by their talent or financial resources are highly unlikely to excel. To do that, they must understand what they can do well, selectively prune their operations, and perhaps seek to leverage their capabilities with those of others to help cause some good things to happen that otherwise aren't likely to happen. Sometimes, though, there might be good reasons for some of them – especially larger organizations - to venture into areas that have not previously been in their comfort zones.

Not surprisingly, I'll use the Indianapolis-based Goodwill as an example. As I mentioned in Chapter 1, Goodwill's territory-based structure tends to foster diversification. If you are prohibited from going beyond certain geographic boundaries and have well developed one phase of your work, you might add another product or service related to your primary mission as a way to grow the organization. A certain amount of that can work and might even improve your overall impact – if you're growing in talent at roughly *the same rate you're growing in size and scope. While in my later years we usually did that pretty well, there were times earlier in my career when we became overly diversified and stretched our resources – especially our management talent - too much (For an example, see the story in Chapter 3 of our numerous entrepreneurial ventures during the recession of the early 1980s.)*

*In 2004, though, we entered the field of public education by opening a public charter high school. While we had never run a school before, over the previous several years we had gained a fair amount of relevant experience through some small-scale initiatives with a local school system. We had also entered into a relationship with a company that had developed the educational model we initially adopted, and we received a lot of help from them. In addition, we had a lot of organizational strength, including a lot of talented people, strong support services and a solid financial position. Without those strengths, I doubt we would have been successful. Even with those strengths, that initiative turned out to be the most difficult of anything we tried in my entire career. Yet, it also turned out to be the catalyst for tremendous organizational learning and a rapid increase in the rate at which our entire organization evolved. It was one of the major turning points in our then-80+ year history.*

*Some of the learning that followed the launch of that first school later resulted in our development of the Excel Center, which is now enabling many thousands of adults in several states to earn a high school diploma.*

*The learning that followed the opening of our first school also led to the decision to implement Nurse-Family Partnership in Indiana, which some people might consider to be another example of mission creep. While we had worked for three years to find a way to bring NFP to Indiana because we thought the state needed it, I had no intention of our trying to run it ourselves. But when the Indiana State Department of Health asked us to do so, I finally consented, believing that to be the only way we would get the program into our state. I also knew we had the infrastructure to support it, and I had confidence we could do it well.*

What I failed to realize at the outset, though, was how good a fit NFP would turn out to be, as we quickly saw the opportunities for synergies with other parts of Goodwill. We could connect the young moms who lacked high school diplomas to the Excel Center, and we could connect them with employment opportunities at Goodwill or with other firms. And because Goodwill had strong relationships with many other organizations, we could connect the NFP families to other services that might be beneficial to them. And as all of this happened, our organization began to take on a different form and a whole-person, two-generation approach evolved.

In the for-profit world, when companies want expertise in fields where they have none, some well-used approaches are to buy, merge or develop a joint venture with another company that has the desired expertise. Those approaches also make sense, but are less frequently used, in the not-for-profit sector. They were not viable options when we were considering launching a charter school, and if we had followed conventional wisdom, we never would have taken that step.

Had that been the case, Goodwill in central Indiana would not have developed the Excel Center or brought NFP to Indiana, and it's doubtful we would have begun to emphasize a whole-person, two-generation approach with many of the people we worked with. The organization would most likely continue to be viewed as somewhat traditional, and I firmly believe its impact would be nowhere nearly as great as it is today. But with the learning and the talent that has been added to the organization since the beginning of that first school, prospects for the future are incredibly exciting – for the organization and its impact in the lives of people.

# CHAPTER 16

## *Forty Years of Learning Summarized on One Chart*

Toward the end of my Goodwill career, I attempted to summarize on one chart the essence of what I had learned about the ingredients necessary to sustain organizational success over a long period of time. Here's a brief explanation of what appears at the end of this piece.

- Every organization exists in a larger context and is affected by many external factors, including changes in the economy, demographics, technology, competition, laws and regulations, the dominant culture in the society, and external shocks, which can be natural or man-made disasters. Organizations must be able to adapt quickly and effectively to such changes or risk becoming ineffective, irrelevant, or extinct.

- It can be useful to keep in mind that, at the most basic level, organizations change for three reasons: They see a need or an opportunity; they have a sense or fear of something that might happen; or they change in response to something that's already happened.

- Components of organizational leadership include governance, management, and aspirations (or vision) as articulated by the leaders, who should begin with the end in mind, i.e., by determining how they will measure success. They should then translate the aspirations into concrete, measurable goals and align everything toward those goals, including organizational structure, business models, products and services, resource development and alloca-tion, recruitment and hiring, training and development, perfor-mance reporting, recognition and reward systems, policies and practices, internal and external communication, and organiza-tional culture. The leaders should be aware that most organiza-tions are perfectly aligned for the results they are getting, and if any major factor is significantly out of alignment, it will be nearly impossible for the organization to excel over time.

- The leaders must also recognize that none of the above is static. Everything is subject to change as new opportunities or challenges arise and as the external environment changes.

- Success of not-for-profit organizations or for-profit social enter-prises is a function of three elements:

  - **Impact**, which is a function of mission-related results. How many people are benefiting, and to what extent are their lives being changed for the better? Measures of real impact are much deeper than activity metrics such as "number of people served," which might indicate you were busy, but tell us nothing about whether you actu-ally made a difference.

  - **Financial sustainability**, which is a function of finan-cial strength. Do you have sufficient strength to be able to weather periodic downturns and occasional external shocks? Do you have enough to invest in initiatives that will enable you to further strengthen your mission-re-lated businesses and services, increase your impact, meet or beat the competition, or respond to changes in your external environment?

- **Adaptability** (or agility), which is a function of the organization's culture. Can you respond quickly and effectively as new needs, opportunities, or threats arise and as the external environment changes?

An organization can be successful for a time with just the first two, but it will cease being so if its culture does not enable it to adapt effectively as the world in which it operates changes.

- A good overall objective for a not-for-profit organization or a for-profit social enterprise is to maximize mission-related impact while maintaining a financial position that enhances long term viability.

- The leaders of a successful organization must constantly be aware that sustained success can lead to succumbing to the demons of inertia, complacency, myopia, or arrogance. They should remind themselves of the old proverb, "Whom the gods would destroy they give forty years of success." Today, though, it doesn't take anywhere near forty years for any of those demons to cause an organization to be destroyed by outside forces or to self-destruct.

- In the final analysis, the most important factor determining the success or failure of an organization is the quality of its leadership. Successful organizations have leadership that:

  - understands its context

  - knows what it wants to accomplish

  - aligns everything toward that end

  - is never content with the status quo

  - and continues to learn, adapt, and evolve

This is one model of the ingredients necessary for sustained organizational success. But it's good to keep in mind George E. P. Box's admonition, "All models are wrong. Some models are useful."

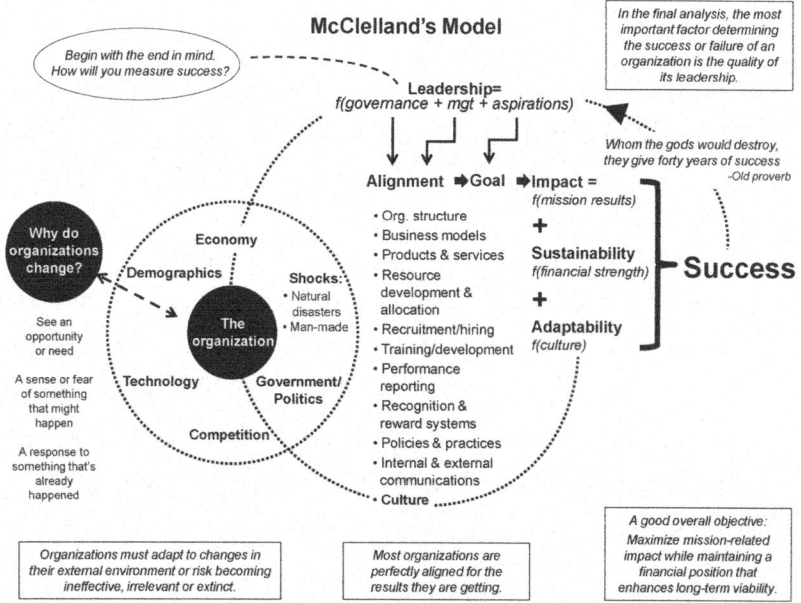

# FOOD FOR THOUGHT

## Fulfilling Our Corporate Social

## Responsibility as an Employer

*(Adapted from a commencement address I gave to graduating students at
the Indiana University Kelley School of Business in Indianapolis in 2012.)*

*A*s CEO, I was acutely aware that nearly two-thirds of our employees at
Goodwill had vocational options that were limited by a disability, criminal history, low education level, or other significant barrier. I also knew that
nearly half of them were the primary source of income in their households.
That placed an enormous responsibility on those of us in leadership positions
to run the organization really well so we could continue to provide a livelihood for all those people who were counting on us. And we did not take that
responsibility lightly.

As leaders, what we do matters. If we're not paying attention to what's
going on around us and we allow ourselves to be blindsided, it matters. If
we become myopic, complacent, or arrogant; if we fail to take care of our
customers; if we fail to recognize what our competition is doing or fail to
see new competitors or new forms of competition that are emerging, it matters. If we don't successfully adapt to changes in our environment - changes
in technology, demographics, the legal or regulatory landscape, or the larger
economy, it matters. Even worse, if we cut corners, act unethically or illegally,
take actions that might benefit us in the short run, but that will eventually
result in long term damage, it matters tremendously. _How_ we go about our
work matters just as much as the work itself. And all these things matter to

*a lot of people who are likely to lose their jobs if those of us who are running the organization aren't doing <u>our</u> jobs as well as we possibly can. And if we let that happen, we should and probably will lose our jobs, too.*

*On the other hand, if as leaders we <u>are</u> paying attention to what's going on around us; if we're recognizing opportunities, trying new ways to grow our businesses and accomplish our mission; if we <u>are</u> operating according to high ethical standards; if we're continuing to learn and adapt; if we're being good stewards of our resources; and if we're treating everyone with respect and providing the kind of workplace and culture that enables our people to grow, we're likely to see our organization grow, evolve, and employ more people. Fortunately, at Goodwill, that was our experience, as we added over 1,000 jobs in central Indiana and increased our revenue by 55% in the last five years of my career.*

*Of course, our experiences weren't always that positive, and no employer can guarantee that any job will last forever. Changes in the external environment occur at an incredible rate and require near constant adaptation. Along the way, some jobs disappear while others are created. Some people learn and adapt to changing circumstances and requirements, others don't.*

*Our approach was to do the best job we could to grow the organization in a financially responsible manner while simultaneously increasing our mission-related impact. In addition, while recognizing that each of us is primarily responsible for continuing to learn all our lives, as an employer, we are often in a position to help our people learn and grow, improve their education, and earn credentials that enhance their future employment prospects. Then, if circumstances beyond the control of an individual result in the loss of a job, at least the person affected is likely to be better prepared for his/her next step than might have been the case otherwise.*

*In my opinion, when an organization is operating in a manner that enhances the prospects it will be able to continue providing a livelihood for its employees, and when that company is doing all it can to help its employees learn and grow, it is exercising what might be considered its most important corporate social responsibility.*

*In the kind of organization we ran, operating in that manner also resulted in what might be considered optimal impact.*

# CLOSING THOUGHTS

## *Second Chances*

*I*t's not unusual to hear someone speak of America as a land of second chances. In this country, most people tend to be reasonably forgiving and willing to give a person another chance – most of the time, at least.

Nor was it unusual for me to hear people at Goodwill talk about how we or someone in our organization gave them a second chance that changed their lives. A few examples:

- A young man who dropped out of school to help support his siblings after their father died told me that without a high school diploma or even any high school credits, he had no future. He enrolled in and graduated from the Excel Center. He said, "I now have a future."

- A young woman on the autism spectrum who had dropped out of school enrolled in an Excel Center. She subsequently became the first person in her family to graduate from high school.

- A mother of five convinced her daughter to enroll in the Excel Center. Shortly thereafter, two of her sons enrolled, and then the mom, who had dropped out of school in the 9th grade, and another family member enrolled. All have now graduated. The mother told me, "Everyone (in the Excel Center) strives to treat everyone with respect – no matter who you are. We are pushed to become the best we can possibly be and to continuously look for ways to grow."

- A *Goodwill retail store employee who has struggled with alcohol abuse told me he had lost everything and no one would hire him – no one, that is, except Goodwill. After six years of employment he continues to do a great job. He said, "Goodwill gave me a chance for a new life."*

- *Another employee told me that when she was hired by Goodwill she had no place to live, no car, no money, and no future. When I talked with her, she was an assistant store manager and nearing completion of requirements for a bachelor's degree in business.*

- *An employee who at the time had been with us one year had been a medical professional before he developed a disability that rendered him unable to do what he had done before. One of our store managers gave him a chance, and he told me he loves working for Goodwill.*

There's another group at Goodwill that is benefiting from a second chance. At the time I retired, over 300 of our employees had come to us with felony records, and many of them had previously had trouble finding an employer who would give them an opportunity to start life anew. Does it always work out? Of course not. But neither does it always work out for the population in general. Most of the time, though, it does. The benefits – to the individuals who have been given a second chance and to the larger society – are huge.

Throughout its history, Goodwill has employed a lot of people few others were willing to hire – whether because of a disability, a criminal history, a low education level, or some other barrier. In many cases, rather than a second chance, Goodwill has given them a first chance to become productive, contributing citizens.

There are limits, of course. While we were always happy to work with those who put forth their best effort and tried to do a good job, those who made it difficult or impossible for us to trust them would seldom find another opportunity in our organization. Neither would those who demonstrated a pattern of treating others poorly.

On the other hand, employees who demonstrated good work habits and a good attitude, treated others in a respectful manner, had a genuine desire to improve their education and skill levels and were willing to put forth the necessary effort to do so often qualified for assistance from Goodwill that would lead to better career opportunities with us or with another employer.

Not long before I stepped down as Goodwill's CEO, I spoke to a room full of 75 new students in one of the Excel Centers. All of them had previously dropped out of high school and were returning to earn their diplomas. It was their second day. One of them asked me how Goodwill got started. As I was telling the story, I mentioned that the founder, Edgar Helms, believed in giving people not charity, but a chance. As soon as I said that, the room erupted in spontaneous loud, sustained applause. Those students weren't looking for handouts. They were looking for opportunity. And I believe there are many thousands more like them – looking for an opportunity for a second chance.

One of Goodwill's historic values is that the organization provides opportunities, not charity, and fosters development, not dependency. That value is just as strong today as it was when Goodwill was founded in the early years of the 20th century – and there are still many who appreciate it, whether they are looking for an opportunity for a first, second, or even a third chance.

# ACKNOWLEDGMENTS

After I retired from Goodwill in April 2015, I spent a lot of time sorting through documents I had written throughout my career and began bringing some of those together in a form that might eventually become a book. About a year later, Lane Schonour, who at the time was Senior Director of Leadership Development for Goodwill Industries International, reviewed the first draft of the manuscript and offered many helpful suggestions. Lane had done his doctoral dissertation on the Indianapolis Goodwill's development of charter schools and, in the process, had become quite familiar with our organization.

One of the questions Lane raised was whether what I was writing should be several smaller pamphlets or more than one book. While I was pondering that and beginning to write a second draft, I was asked to help lead the State of Indiana's response to the opioid crisis. Work on the book stopped for the next three years.

Serving as Indiana's "drug czar" was a tremendous experience that provided some new insights for me. A lot of what we had learned during the latter part of my Goodwill career about how to reduce multigenerational poverty was just as applicable in reducing substance abuse and helping people with a substance use disorder achieve and maintain recovery. But I also learned a lot more and gained some (for me) new insights into approaches we, as a society, might take to substantially reduce some serious social problems.

After I left my position at the Statehouse and entered my second retirement, I began writing again. I still tried to incorporate everything into one book and asked a longtime friend, Jerry Davis, to critique my manuscript. Jerry told me a lot that I needed to hear, including that I was trying to cram too much into one book. I listened, then wrote *Toward Greater Impact – A Path to Reducing Social Problems, Improving Lives, and Strengthening Communities.*

Following the publication of that book in May 2021, I began working on this book. Once again, I asked Jerry to critique the first draft. He offered many suggestions, most of which I incorporated into the next draft. He has been enormously helpful, and I'm grateful to him.

Kent Kramer, Ivan Cropper, and Jenny Kakasuleff at Goodwill of Central and Southern Indiana also reviewed the manuscript and made several helpful comments and suggestions. They are also the source of some of the stories I've included in the book, and I'm deeply grateful to them.

Finally, as always, I'm grateful to my wife, Jane, for tolerating my spending so much of my time in my second retirement writing. Because this period of our lives has coincided with the Covid-19 pandemic, at least we weren't foregoing travel, which has not been a good option for us during the past 1-1/2 years. Along with millions of others, though, we look forward to the day when we can more fully resume some of the activities we have enjoyed so much in years past.

# ABOUT THE AUTHOR

In 2015 Jim McClelland concluded a 45-year career as an executive with Goodwill Industries. Forty-one of those years were as President and CEO of one of the largest and most diversified Goodwill organizations in the country, based in Indianapolis. Following his Goodwill career, he served three years as Executive Director for Drug Prevention, Treatment, and Enforcement for the State of Indiana.

Jim has served on the boards of numerous not-for-profit organizations at local, national, and international levels and chaired several of them. He was also heavily involved in helping develop Goodwill Industries in South Korea.

Among other honors, Jim has been inducted into the Central Indiana Business Hall of Fame, the Georgia Tech Engineering Hall of Fame, and the Goodwill Industries International Hall of Fame. He is also a recipient of the Distinguished Entrepreneur Award from the Kelley School of Business at Indiana University and the Lifetime Achievement in Innovation Award from the Venture Club of Indiana.

Jim earned a bachelor's degree in Industrial Engineering at Georgia Tech and an MBA from the Kelley School of Business at Indiana University. He enjoys reading and travel and has visited all 50 states and all seven continents.

A native of Florida, Jim and his wife, Jane, live in Indianapolis. They have two grown children and two grandchildren.